Empowering

T0290584

Community-Wide Strategic Planning in
Rock Hill, South Carolina

Craig M. Wheeland

University Press of America,® Inc.
Dallas · Lanham · Boulder · New York · Oxford

Copyright © 2004 by
University Press of America,® Inc.
4501 Forbes Boulevard
Suite 200
Lanham, Maryland 20706
UPA Acquisitions Department (301) 459-3366

PO Box 317
Oxford
OX2 9RU, UK

Library of Congress Control Number: 2003116037
ISBN 0-7618-2827-3 (paperback : alk. ppr.)

⊖™ The paper used in this publication meets the minimum
requirements of American National Standard for Information
Sciences—Permanence of Paper for Printed Library Materials,
ANSI Z39.48—1984

To my wife, Anne
And our Children, Lucy and Ryan

Contents

Tables and Illustrations   vii

Preface ix

Acknowledgements   xi

Chapter 1 Community-Wide Strategic Planning and
                    Urban Regime Theory   1

Chapter 2 The Basic Design of Empowering the Vision   13

Chapter 3 Lessons from the Planning Process: 1987 to 1989   29

Chapter 4 Achieving the Vision: ETV Ten Years Later   45

Chapter 5 Political Factions and Regime Formation   65

Chapter 6 Conflict, Cooperation and Issue-Based Politics   85

Chapter 7 Using Community-Wide Strategic Planning in
                    The Future   103

Appendix Research Design   109

Endnotes   115

Bibliography   131

Index   143

About the Author   149

Tables and Illustrations

Tables

2.1 ETV Steering Committee Members

2.2 ETV Co-Chairs of Theme Groups

3.1 Community Organizations Represented in ETV

3.2 Theme Group Participants by Political Party

3.3 Theme Group Participants by Gender

3.4 Theme Group Participants by Race

3.5 Theme Group Participants by Occupation

3.6 Theme Group Participants by Ward

4.1 ETC Steering Committee Members

4.2 Theme Group Participants' Views of Their Experiences in ETV and/or ETC

4.3 Theme Group Participants' Views of Their Experiences by Initiative

4.4 Steering Committee and Planning Staff Views of Sponsors' Contributions to ETV/ETC Processes and Implementation

5.1 Business and Civic Leaders Supporting Progressive Initiatives

5.2 Assessment of City Services

5.3 Spending Preferences on City Services

A.1 Gender and Race of 124 ETV and 176 ETC Participants and the 113 ETV/ETC Participants Responding to the Survey

A.2 Occupation of 124 ETV and 176 ETC Participants and the 113 ETV/ETC Participants Responding to the Survey

A.1 Political Party of 124 ETV and 176 ETC Participants and the 113 ETV/ETC Participants Responding to the Survey

Illustrations

2.1 ETV Endorsement Resolution: City Version

Preface

This book grew out of my opportunities to observe Rock Hill's "Empowering the Vision (ETV)," the name given to the community-wide strategic planning initiative. I moved to Rock Hill, South Carolina in August 1987 to begin my job as member of Winthrop College's political science department. I lived there until August 1990 at which time I moved to Pennsylvania. My time in Rock Hill allowed me to observe many of the events related to ETV and to attend some of them as well. I did not have any formal role in the planning process.

By observing and researching the ETV process as it occurred, rather than participating, I maintained my independent view point. Had the ETV initiative in the late 1980s failed to be completed, as was the case for many other cities, then writing about Rock Hill would be less interesting to scholars and local government professionals; instead of failure, Rock Hill completed the ETV planning process in the late 1980s using standard and unique features that deserved to be studied.

In 1990 I joined the faculty at Villanova University. I followed Rock Hill's progress throughout the 1990s by visiting the city's web site, reading on-line articles in *The Herald*, and visiting the city in 1995. I returned to Rock Hill for extensive field work in September 1999 as part of my follow-up study to see how the plan had been implemented. My participation in the Rock Hill Economic Development Corporation's retreat in November 1999 was a direct result of my having initiated the follow-up study. The retreat featured a retrospective on how community-wide strategic planning had affected the city. I was invited to speak about my preliminary findings. My participation in the retreat gave me more chances to gather relevant information about the Rock Hill effort. I found that the implementation of ETV achieved many of the results promised by advocates of community-wide strategic planning. Rock Hill's ETV is indeed a "best practice" worth studying and modeling.

Craig M. Wheeland
Villanova, Pennsylvania
October 1, 2003

Acknowledgements

Many people have made this book possible. First and foremost, the people of Rock Hill, who gave me so much of their time, have my respect and appreciation. I had unfettered access to community leaders and municipal records. Mayor Betty Jo Rhea, Mayor Doug Echols, City Manager Joe Lanford and City Manager Russell Allen were especially instrumental in helping me do the research for this project. Second, I want to thank my graduate students who worked as my assistants to help do the difficult tasks of coding surveys, entering data in SPSS, preparing endnotes, among others jobs: well done Mary Murphy, Melisa Marcovitz and Julie E. Botsch. Third, I am indebted to Villanova employees, Diane Mozzone, Gail Raiburn and Rachel Schaller, for their expert advice while I prepared the camera-ready manuscript. Fourth, I owe Anne Minicozzi, my wife, at least one vacation at the beach for her careful editing of the manuscript. Finally, I would like to thank the American Political Science Association for partially funding the research in 1999 by awarding me a grant via the Small Research Grant Program for faculty at non-doctoral granting institutions.

Three chapters in this book have appeared as articles in three distinguished journals. Most of Chapter 2 appeared as "Empowering the Vision: Citywide Strategic Planning." *National Civic Review* 80 (Fall): 393-405 (copyright 1991 by National Civic League, Inc.; reprinted by permission of National Civic League and Jossey-Bass.). Chapter 3 appeared as "Citywide Strategic Planning: An Evaluation of Rock Hill's Empowering the Vision." *Public Administration Review* 53(1): 65-72 (copyright 1993 by The American Society for Public Administration; reprinted by permission of The American Society for Public Administration.). Chapter 4 appeared as "Implementing a Community-Wide Strategic Plan: Rock Hill's Empowering the Vision Ten Years Later." *The American Review of Public Administration.* 33:1 (March): 46-69 (copyright 2003 by Sage Publications; reprinted by permission of Sage Publications.).

Chapter 1

Community-Wide Strategic Planning and Urban Regime Theory

Future research should also explore the types of policies and politics that are possible within the various arenas.

- Barbara Ferman

Confronted by economic, social and political change of a large magnitude in the 1980s, many cities across the United States decided to use community-wide strategic planning as a tool to address their problems and to take advantage of any opportunities these changes presented.[1] John Bryson defines strategic planning as a "disciplined effort to produce fundamental decisions and actions that shape and guide what an organization (or other entity) is, what it does, and why it does it."[2] Or as Gerald Gordon suggests, it "is a process by which an organization attempts to control its destiny rather than allowing future events to do so."[3] A community-wide strategic planning process involves citizens and organizations from the public, for-profit and not-for-profit sectors that have a stake in the community. Because of its intersectoral and intergovernmental character, extensive citizen participation, and visioning component, community-wide strategic planning is the most difficult type of planning to do well.

This book describes and analyzes how Rock Hill, South Carolina used community-wide strategic planning successfully to develop a ten-year plan, and to implement many features in that plan during the 1990s. Rock Hill named its process Empowering the Vision (ETV) and later the ten-year plan itself came to be known as ETV. Rock Hill is located within the Charlotte, North Carolina Metropolitan Statistical Area (MSA). The city's population in 2000 was 49,765, with 37 percent African American.[4] Why Rock Hill was one of a few cities to achieve significant results using this type of planning is explained by reviewing the city's competent use of this tool, the leadership provided by key individuals, and especially by studying Rock Hill's politics. The city's public officials used community-wide strategic planning as a tool to expand the purposes of Rock Hill's urban regime and to construct the coalition capable of implementing the plan. Rock Hill's experiences also help us understand how many southern cities in the United States tried to adjust to the social and economic changes affecting their region since the 1960s. The lessons learned from Rock Hill's successful effort can provide guidance to other communities as they use this planning tool, and contribute to the development and testing of theories of community-building and governance.

Coping with Economic and Social Change

Rock Hill began as a train depot, post office and shopping district in the 1850s .[5] In 1870 this settlement incorporated as a town and then became a city in 1892. Rock Hill was the second city in South Carolina to adopt the council-manager form of government and employed its first city manager in 1915. The city attracted its first textile mill in the 1880s when this industry began to invest in the Piedmont region of the South, which David Goldfield defines as a region that "extended south from Richmond; widened to encompass the area between Raleigh and Charlotte in North Carolina; narrowed through Spartanburg, Greenville, and Anderson in South Carolina; continued on through Atlanta; and culminated in the Appalachian foothills south of what became Birmingham, Alabama."[6] In 1895 Rock Hill also became the permanent home of Winthrop College, which at that time was a state-supported college for women.   Clinton Junior College serving primarily the African American community was founded in 1894.   Although the presence of these colleges did help diversify the city's economy, the textile industry was the main engine driving the city's economic growth from the 1880s through the 1970s.[7]

Like many southern cities, Rock Hill experienced dramatic change in the 1970s and 1980s. Deindustrialization swept through the

Piedmont region as the textile industry "cut more than 300,000 jobs between 1979 and 1985" in the face of foreign competition.[8] Rock Hill lost its textile industry and subsequently also experienced the economic decline, indeed near complete abandonment, of its downtown business district. Unlike the small, one-industry towns located in the Piedmont that "shut down" when the mills closed,[9] Rock Hill's location as a suburban *ring city* in the rapidly growing Charlotte MSA attracted new economic development. Although the city's leaders recognized their location advantage and welcomed new economic growth in the 1980s, many were displeased with the pattern of urban sprawl it produced. New businesses located in the undeveloped areas within the city, especially along the roads connecting the city to major highways, rather than in the downtown business district. Many city leaders preferred a pattern of well-planned, balanced, high-quality economic development. Furthermore, the economic development occurring within the area between Rock Hill and Charlotte began to reduce the open space that had separated the two cities physically and also psychologically. Rock Hill's proximity to Charlotte also attracted an influx of new residents, many of them from other regions of the United States, changing the character of the population.

These economic and demographic changes challenged Rock Hill's identity as a stable, "textile community" of long-term residents. They also presented an opportunity to re-build and to re-define the city's identity. City leaders worried that without a buffer separating Charlotte from their community, without a vibrant downtown, and without an effort to preserve the   city's history and culture, Rock Hill would become a "typical suburb" lacking a unique identity. In his conclusions about the loss of community in metropolitan America, Kenneth Jackson captures the fear motivating many Rock Hill leaders: "In our time, most observers have noted that alienation and *anomie* are more characteristic of urban life than a sense of participation and belonging."[10] Although many of the small, one-industry towns hurt by the textile industry's decline lacked the ability to form "development coalitions consisting of government, business and education" that might take advantage of new economic opportunities and adjust to social change,[11] Rock Hill was in the position to do so.

The Origin of ETV

During the Fall of 1987 Mayor Betty Jo Rhea and City Manager Joe Lanford initiated the idea of doing a two-year long community-wide strategic planning process through a series of informal meetings of city officials and community leaders and a retreat sponsored by the Rock Hill Chamber of Commerce. These talks laid the foundation Lanford needed to develop ETV's basic design, which is discussed thoroughly in Chapter 2. Seven community institutions agreed to sponsor ETV and to send representatives to serve on the steering committee: the City of Rock Hill, York County, Rock Hill School District No. 3, Rock Hill Chamber of Commerce, York Technical College, Winthrop College (now Winthrop University), and the Rock Hill Economic Development Corporation (RHEDC). ETV's steering committee began meeting in January 1988. Citizens were invited to serve on six theme groups: Garden City, Business City, Functional City, Educational City, Cultural City and Historic City. Rock Hill used ETV to answer three main questions: Will Rock Hill become just another suburb that looks like Anywhere, USA?; Can Rock Hill avoid this fate by defining a new identity for itself in the Charlotte MSA?; How can Rock Hill enhance the quality-of-life of its residents? The planning process ended in September 1989 with the presentation of the plan to the public and to a regional conference of municipal leaders in Charlotte, NC.

Rock Hill produced a ten year plan intended to change the city into a *Southern urban village on the leading edge of Charlotte*. ETV combined an economic development strategy that featured using the city-supported RHEDC to build business parks and essentially buy downtown in order to redevelop it, and a social development strategy that featured art, history and culture. ETV's plan included an emphasis on public art, historic preservation, gardens, green-ways, cultural events, business park development, housing, infrastructure improvements, and downtown office development. This approach to using history as a development tool is consistent with the approach larger southern cities, such as Charleston, Savannah, New Orleans, and Richmond, used in the 1970s.[12] Indeed, Rock Hill leaders hoped to position the city as the most desirable "out-town" location, to use Goldfield's term, in the Charlotte MSA.[13] The implementation of the ten-year plan began officially in January 1990.

Celebrating and Revising ETV

Mid-way through the ten-year implementation period, in April 1995, Rock Hill began a new community-wide strategic planning process to review ETV's accomplishments and update the plan. After much discussion, the steering committee decided to change the name of the planning process from ETV to Empowering the Community (ETC) in order to reflect the new emphasis on neighborhood empowerment.[14] The plan produced by ETC included many initiatives carried over from ETV and new ones as well. Implementation of ETC's plan began officially in January 1997.

Significance of the Rock Hill Case

When Rock Hill initiated ETV, community-wide strategic planning was still a new and somewhat unproven tool to use. Several sources published in the 1980s documented how to use strategic planning in local government.[15] A few other cities were using strategic planning with some success.[16] Theodore Poister and Gregory Streib found in their survey of cities with a population over 25,000 in the United States that a majority of cities in all regions of the United States, but especially in the West and North Central regions, used strategic planning within "selected areas," (e.g., public works).[17] However, they also found that fewer than 25 percent of cities attempted to use strategic planning on a community-wide basis. Poister and Streib concluded that strategic planning "may be seen as more useful for major organizational units with a unified sense of mission rather than a highly diversified and fragmented municipal jurisdiction as a whole."[18] In a 1990 survey of cities with a population over 100,000, Carmen Scavo reported that only 16 percent of cities used strategic planning to foster citizen participation.[19] In the 1980s, John Bryson and William Roering studied the efforts to produce a strategic plan in eight governmental units, five of which were cities.[20] After finding that only one of the five cities in their study completed all steps in the strategic planning process, and only three of the five cities adopted at least some parts of their strategic plans, Bryson and Roering concluded that "most efforts to produce fundamental decisions and policy changes in government through strategic planning will not succeed . . . . Strategic Planning is no panacea."[21]

The evidence discussed in Chapter 3 indicates Rock Hill became a successful early user of community-wide strategic planning, especially among southern cities. The city overcame the barriers to success and provided an example of how this tool could be used to develop a ten-year plan. ETV not only incorporated many standard features of a strategic planning process, but used innovative features as well. Rock Hill's success rested on nine features:

(1) maintaining strong, stable public leadership (especially the

mayor and city manager);
(2) a commitment of sufficient public resources;
(3) securing the involvement of key institutions as stakeholders/sponsors;
(4) finding strong process champions to guide the planning effort;
(5) employing consultants as educators and therefore avoiding a consultant dominated effort;
(6) using creative work processes in a highly symbolic setting;
(7) creating physical models and computer-generated images to help visualize the effects of the plan;
(8) securing broad-based citizen participation; and
(9) endorsing ETV as a "living" plan that will be monitored and updated over the ten year period.

Rock Hill won three awards for ETV: the 1989 Planning Award from the South Carolina Association of American Planners, the 1990 Municipal Association of South Carolina Achievement Award, and was one of five cities receiving the 1992 U.S. Conference of Mayors Livability Award for cities with populations under 100,000.[22]

During the 1990s, using strategic planning on a community-wide basis became more popular, especially among cities with populations greater than 100,000.[23] By the late 1990s, Gregory Streib and Theodore Poister reported that 24 percent of cities with populations over 25,000 completed one or more community-wide plans and southern cities were now more likely to do so than cities in other regions.[24] They also reported that the large majority of these cities believed they achieved numerous beneficial results, such as "focusing the council's agenda on important issues, communicating with citizens groups and external stakeholders, and maintaining public support."[25] Did the implementation of Rock Hill's ETV achieve its promise, or is it another example of a well intentioned, but later abandoned use of strategic planning? Informed by the literature on public sector strategic planning, collaborative decision-making and governance theory, I use five important results to determine if Rock Hill successfully implemented ETV:

(1) the effective management of uncertainty by promoting learning, especially about environmental (i.e., contextual) conditions;
(2) the resolution of conflict by facilitating goal agreement among the participants;

(3) the continued participation of citizens representative of the community;

(4) the achievement of tangible and intangible results; and

(5) the establishment of a governance network for the community which remains operational for at least the duration of the planning period (i.e., ten years in Rock Hill's case).

In Chapter 4, the evidence is presented indicating Rock Hill achieved these results. Why Rock Hill succeeded when other cities have not is best explained by studying Rock Hill's politics.

An Overview of Urban Regime Theory

Urban regime theory became popular in the 1980s as an approach to explaining city politics that moved past the decades old community power debate between elitists and pluralists,[26] as well as the structuralist's view emphasizing class struggle.[27] Urban regime theory offers an account of how governmental power can combine with social and economic power to govern cities. Regimes are formed by leaders of organizations from the public and private sectors who allocate their organizations' resources to implement a shared agenda for action. Clarence Stone defines an urban regime as "the informal arrangements by which public bodies and private interests function together in order to be able to make and carry out governing decisions."[28] It is this ability to produce rather than the power to control all major decisions that enables an urban regime to govern.[29] As Richard DeLeon explains "urban regimes are powerful because they are empowering. They provide citizens and their government leaders with the 'power to' undertake complex objectives and solve social problems in a politically granulated and gridlocked world."[30]

The nature of an urban regime will vary across cities and within a particular city over time. They are, as Stone suggests, "dynamic, not static."[31]   Robert Pecorella explores the life cycle of urban regimes suggesting that a regime's duration is affected by "the evolution of normal politics incrementally" as new groups are accommodated, and especially by fiscal crises, which "abruptly change the nature of urban regimes by destabilizing existing governing coalitions and forcing . . . non-incremental adjustments in public policy."[32] He adapts Anthony Downs' life cycle approach to explaining the development of bureaucracy to explaining urban regime stability and change. Pecorella suggests "the evolution of regime behavior can be viewed as a series of stages representing a regime's life cycle, including periods of regime initiation, regime consolidation, regime fragmentation, and regime demise."[33] Several other scholars have developed typologies of regimes in order to better understand regime variation.

H. V. Savitch and John Clayton Thomas use the strength o f political leadership (strong or weak) and the unity of the business elite (cohesive or dispersed) to develop four types of urban regimes: corporatist (strong/cohesive), elitist (weak/cohesive), pluralist (strong/dispersed), and hyperpluralist (weak/dispersed).[34] Deleon adds the concept of the "anti-regime" as a transitional type of political order that may follow the demise of the old regime.[35] The "anti-regime" has the power to stop action, but has not formed into a new coalition capable of moving from the chaos of the "wild city" (or extreme hyperpluralism) to the stability of a new regime. Finally, Clarence Stone, Marion Orr, and David Imbroscio categorize regimes based on the kind of initiatives they pursue and the kind of resources needed to implement their agendas.[36] The successful regime is one that has "a capacity to mobilize resources commensurate with the requirements of its main policy agenda."[37]

Stone, Orr and Imbroscio identify four types of regimes: caretaker, redevelopment, middle-class progressive, and lower-class opportunity expansion.[38] Stone, Orr and Imbroscio suggest that "because actual regimes may be mixtures of the types described here, cities predominately of one kind may display tendencies toward another type."[39]

A caretaker regime maintains the provision of routine services and therefore can rely on "periodic popular approval at the ballot box" in order to mobilize sufficient resources to implement its limited agenda.[40]

A redevelopment regime seeks to promote business development, especially in the central business district, through the provision of subsidies and other government supported inducements. A redevelopment regime requires the mobilization of various elites, including "real estate and developer interests, financial institutions, newspapers, utilities, and other large downtown property owners who have a major stake in the enhancement of land values in the central city; . . . [and who] have the resources to devote to the cultivation of a favorable political climate as well as the technical expertise and financial capacity to promote development."[41]

A middle-class progressive regime supports "historic preservation, environmental protection, affordable housing to preserve and promote diversity, affirmative action in employment and business contracts, and linkage funds for various social purposes."[42] This type of regime requires the mobilization of middle-class activists who are independent of business/corporate interests and can rely upon "a base of active popular support" to implement their agenda.[43]

The lower-class opportunity expansion regime seeks ways to "expand opportunities for the lower class through the enhancement of human capital and widened access to employment and ownership."[44] Establishing and sustaining such a regime is very difficult because it requires the mobilization of the urban lower class, which "lacks the organization and other resources to make an opportunity-expanding regime feasible. . . ."[45] Community leaders working to form this type of regime face the greatest obstacles to success.

Barbara Ferman contributes to our understanding of urban regimes by studying the context in which regimes are formed.[46] Ferman's contextual analysis builds on the study of agenda formation and coalition building. It draws our attention to the institutions and the political culture that shapes the behavior of leaders in a particular city as they prepare agendas and form coalitions. Ferman pursues a contextual analysis by using the concept of urban arenas to explain the variation of regime types across cities.[47] She defines urban arenas as the "spheres of activity that are distinguished by particular institutional frameworks and underlying political cultures that lend a structure to these activities."[48] Examples of local government arenas are electoral, civic, intergovernmental and business.

Ferman argues that the particular institutions forming the regime and their way of operating will depend "largely on which arena is the primary home of the activity."[49] She illustrates her point by comparing civic and electoral arenas: "Civic arenas tend to be dominated by private, nonprofit institutions that distribute resources on a collective basis and foster a cooperative culture. Electoral arenas are often dominated by partisan institutions that distribute resources on a market exchange basis and, in so doing, create highly competitive environments."[50] By adding a contextual analysis, Ferman can explain variations within regime types developed by other scholars. For example, in her study of Chicago and Pittsburgh's "growth machines," she found that Pittsburgh's reliance on the civic arena made its leaders receptive to using planning and involving neighborhood groups; in contrast, Chicago's reliance on the electoral arena made its leaders resist neighborhood mobilization and incorporation into the regime.[51]

Rock Hill's Pluralist Regime

Since the late 1960s, the pluralist regime formed by public officials primarily using the electoral arena has governed Rock Hill. The business, civic, and intergovernmental arenas were of secondary importance to regime formation and maintenance. Rock Hill has not had a business leader with the stature of Richard K. Mellon, the financier Ferman described as the man who wielded his financial power and used his network of personal relationships on corporate b oards t o c reate a unified approach to the redevelopment of Pittsburgh.[52] Lacking a dominant business leader, Rock Hill's Chamber of Commerce served as the organization representing business interests in Rock Hill. The Chamber was most effective in the mid-1980s in mobilizing business interests on behalf of several important initiatives, such as the formation of the RHEDC and business support for ETV. The Chamber's membership at that time consisted of about 665 businesses and about 1,300 individual members.[53] Yet even in the mid-1980s, the Chamber was reacting to ideas recommended by public officials (see below). Aside from those few years, differences among developers, and differences between downtown business interests and business interests located in other commercial areas in the city, inhibited collective action. In the 1990s, the Chamber's leaders decided to avoid taking positions on many issues because of differences within its membership.

In contrast to the lack of cohesion among business leaders, Rock Hill's public officials have been well positioned to be the catalysts to any public-private coordinated effort to address the issues confronting the community. They provided the leadership in the intergovernmental, business, and civic arenas. First, city officials were the key leaders who tried to build intergovernmental relationships with York County and with Rock Hill's school district. And they used various national and state grant programs t o help finance a variety of projects, including TownCenter Mall, walking trails, public parks, business parks, an arts center, affordable housing, and expanding recycling programs. Second, city officials also were responsible for securing the support of some business leaders in the Chamber of Commerce in 1983 to create the RHEDC. The RHEDC is a non-profit organization that became the main agent promoting Rock Hill's economic revitalization from 1983 to the present day. Third, city officials were the champions of using community-wide strategic planning as a tool to build the intergovernmental and public-private partnerships, as well as secure the public support, needed to carry-out a broad agenda under the redevelopment/middle-class progressive regime in the 1990s.

In Chapter 5 and Chapter 6, I discuss the evidence indicating how city officials used planning to alter the electoral arena in order to gain support for expanding the regime's purpose. The strength of the pluralist regime has varied over time as political leadership has been affected by electoral politics, but it remains intact as of 2001. And the pluralist regime's purpose has evolved from pursuing primarily a redevelopment agenda in the 1970s and 1980s to a hybrid redevelopment/middle-class progressive agenda from 1989 to 2001.

The Future

In the conclusion to her book, *Challenging the Growth Machine*, Ferman asks: "Can the electoral arena be modified so that it becomes a suitable vehicle for planning?"[54] Her study of Chicago, a city governed by a regime founded in the electoral arena, suggests this will be difficult. Rock Hill is a case of a city governed by a regime founded in the electoral arena that used planning as a tool to alter the regime's purpose. The city's leadership consistently championed the use of this tool and worked to implement the plans produced via community-wide strategic planning. Without this sustained public commitment, Rock Hill would not have been able to shape its future in ways that improved the quality-of-life of its residents and enhanced a tradition of community involvement. Other cities may choose to use community-wide strategic planning if a number of successful applications by risk-taking cities show them how it can be done well. Rock Hill invested the time and money needed to use this tool skillfully. And the city's progressive officials practiced the kind of strategic leadership needed to maintain the coalition capable of implementing much of their vision.

Chapter 2

The Basic Design of Empowering the Vision

> *Because every planning process should be tailored to fit specific situations, every process in practice will be a hybrid.*
>
> - John M. Bryson

The history of municipal government reform includes numerous examples of the application of business models and methods to municipal government design and management. In the 1980s, strategic planning became another of the techniques borrowed from the private sector. Municipal officials were encouraged in the 1980s to use strategic planning as a tool to manage the change and complexity present in their environmental contexts.[1] Even skeptics who thought it was a passing fad recommended using strategic planning at least while it was popular so planners could play a leading role in their communities.[2]

The selective focus on the future is the core idea in strategic planning. Beyond acceptance of this principle, no single approach dominated in the private or public sector. In the 1988 edition of his book, *Strategic Planning for Public and Nonprofit Organizations*, Bryson reviews nine distinct approaches used by corporate planners in the private sector that could guide communities like Rock Hill, who were considering preparing a strategic plan.[3] There were several models offered for use in the public sector as well.[4] Douglas Eadie believed the variety of approaches to strategic planning in both the private and public sectors was to be expected.[5] He argued:

> ... [the] successful application [of strategic planning] is a matter of careful tailoring to the unique circumstances of a particular public organization. While there are themes, to be sure, tying all public sector organizations together, the variations are often crucial to success in planning design. A boilerplate approach, in short, is likely to prove inadequate, if not fatal, and the organization that knows itself well and adapts its planning approaches accordingly is far more likely to experience success in planning.[6]

ETV incorporated the basic steps in strategic planning, but also introduced features unique to Rock Hill. City Manager Lanford and his planning staff developed the structure of ETV, which consisted of nine main components: the initial agreement, the steering committee, the theme groups, the ETV staff, special events, *charettes*, models, the general public, and the timetable.

The Initial Agreement

In contrast to the public planners' perspectives reviewed by Jerome Kaufman and Harvey Jacobs, which suggested that strategic planning was not needed in a city with a strong planning capacity, the Rock Hill planning staff and City Manager Lanford were strong advocates of the tool.[7] Joe Lanford, who was appointed city manager in 1979, is perhaps the main reason why the city maintained a strong planning capability. He had a bachelor's degree in city planning and a master's degree in public administration. Lanford began his career working as a planner and had over 15 years of planning experience before becoming city manager in 1979. During the 1980s, Lanford created a strong planning staff to support his belief that planning can make a vital contribution to city policymaking.

It is not surprising in light of this planning tradition that Rock Hill decided to develop six focal point plans in 1982 as way to respond to the changes occurring in key areas around the city.[8] By 1987 the city completed four focal point plans: the York Tech area, the Cherry Park area, the Herlong/Ebenezer Road area and the Crawford Road area. The two remaining focal point areas to be studied were the downtown area and the Winthrop College area.

Rather than completing these two studies, the city officials, particularly Lanford and Mayor Betty Jo Rhea, began to talk with other community leaders, especially Martha Kime Piper, President of Winthrop College, about the possibility of joining together to develop plans for the city. These plans would include not only a concern for the downtown and the Winthrop College area, but also would address the more fundamental question concerning Rock Hill's identity as a suburban city in the Charlotte MSA. Since several other key community institutions were in the initial stages of developing long-range plans in 1987, including the Chamber of Commerce, Winthrop College, York County and Rock Hill School District No. 3, the opportunity existed to get these various institutions to combine their planning processes.

City officials used a series of informal meetings with leaders of these community institutions to introduce the idea of doing a community-wide strategic plan. These informal discussions led to an opportunity in the Fall of 1987 to discuss the topic at a retreat sponsored by the Rock Hill Chamber of Commerce in Asheville, North Carolina. Most observers give City Manager Lanford credit for having the foresight to expand the focal point plans to include a strategic theme, and for securing the involvement of private, public and nonprofit organizations to sponsor planning initiative.

The Steering Committee

The steering committee consisted of two representatives from each of the seven sponsoring organizations (see Table 2.1). City Manager Lanford and Mayor Rhea represented the city. The committee formally began meeting in January 1988. The steering committee's primary responsibilities included:

(1) monitoring the work of the various theme groups;
(2) preparing a final report;
(3) securing the endorsement of each sponsoring institution;
(4) coordinating the implementation of the plan; and
(5) revising the plan as the need arose in the future.[9]

Table 2.1   ETV Steering Committee Members

Institution	Representatives
City of Rock Hill	Elizabeth D. Rhea, Mayor Joe Lanford, City Manager
Rock Hill School District No. 3	Ted Melton, Chairman Joe Gentry, Superintendent
Rock Hill Chamber of Commerce	Marty Cope, President Bill Neely, Past President
RHEDC	Bob Belk, Chairman Jim Reese, Staff
York Technical College	Andy Carter, Chairman Baxter Hood, President[1] Dennis Merrell, President
Winthrop College	Martha Kime Piper, President[2] Michael Smith, Vice President Becky McMillan, Vice President
York County	David Vipperman, Councilman Gene Klugh, County Manager

[1]Dennis Merrell replaced Baxter Hood during the ETV process;
[2]Martha Kime Piper died during the ETV process.

The steering committee endorsed the following mission statement supporting ETV:

> To prepare a physical development plan for central Rock Hill and a strategic plan for the entire community that will capitalize on the strengths of Rock Hill and result in quality growth that will provide our citizens with opportunities to improve their quality of life.[10]

The Six Theme Groups

Six theme groups were created: Business City, Educational City, Cultural City, Garden City, Historic City and Functional City. The themes were based on the city staff's research on major trends, issues, problems and opportunities influencing Rock Hill. The six theme groups were designed to serve as the mechanism for producing a plan. Two co-chairs appointed by the steering committee guided the work of the theme groups (see Table 2.2). Members of each group were supposed to study their area, identify issues and develop a plan to "take advantage of [Rock Hill's] assets and overcome its liabilities thereby assuring quality development."[11] Members were not supposed to be concerned about the feasibility of their *dreams*. The potential costs of the possible projects were not supposed to prevent the theme groups from discussing or proposing them.[12] In fact the city staff did not develop cost estimates of the proposals until after the two year process had been completed.

About 124 citizens were invited to serve on these groups, and any one interested in serving also was permitted to participate. The initial list of invitees was prepared through an informal, brainstorming process involving Mayor Rhea, City Manager Lanford, members of the steering committee and other members of the city government. The general goal was to attract a representative group of civic leaders, especially regarding race and gender, who shared an interest in making Rock Hill a better place to live, and who had particular expertise in one of the six theme areas. Once the groups were formed, the membership was encouraged to invite other citizens to join them. The overriding concern shaping the selection process was to find people who were civic-minded. People perceived to be too narrow, too critical, or lacking in a commitment to Rock Hill were not invited, but no one was formally excluded if they wanted to participate.

The Empowering the Vision Staff

Four types of staff positions were created to assist the theme groups: the technical advisory staff, the graphics staff, the communication staff and the project coordinator. Theme groups were assigned a technical advisor, a graphics staff member and a communication staff member. The city provided 15 of the 20 staff positions, although initially one of the technical advisors was from the Catawba Regional Planning Council and one of the graphics staff was from Winthrop College. The latter two people gave up their staff positions, because those positions demanded too much of their time. Clearly the city was the primary sponsor of ETV.

Table 2.2   ETV Co-Chairs of Theme Groups

Group	Co-Chairs	Occupation
Garden City	Harry Dalton	Business Executive
	Charlie Scoville	Homemaker
Business City	Lynn Campbell	Engineer/Business
	Bob Thompson	Business Executive
Historic City	Grazier Rhea	Planner
	Johnny Gill	Insurance Agent
Functional City	Bob Mallaney	Engineer/Business
	Wayne Wingate	Executive, *The Herald*
Educational City	Clarence Hornsby	Business Executive
	Charles Corley	Winthrop Professor
Cultural City	Marshall Doswell	Business Executive
	Vicki Huggins Cook	Director of Arts Council

The technical advisory staff consisted of planners working for the city directly or working for the RHEDC, a non-profit organization primarily staffed by the city. Their main tasks were (1) preparing agendas for meetings, (2) providing supporting research on the city's strengths and weaknesses, (3) providing information on the various alternatives, (4) arranging site visits and guest speakers, and (5) following-up on work needed from the graphics staff.

The graphics staff consisted of three city employees and three interns specifically hired by the city to work on ETV. The graphics staff members each were assigned to two theme groups. Their main responsibilities were to help the theme groups visualize ideas and also to generate ideas for solving the problems raised by the theme group members.

The communication staff was responsible for (1) maintaining the minutes of the theme group meetings, (2) mailing the minutes and other information to the theme group members and (3) keeping the project coordinator informed about the theme group's activities and progress. The communication staff consisted of two city employees and one person each from Winthrop College, York County, Rock Hill School District No. 3 and the Chamber of Commerce.

The project coordinator was the one person responsible for the entire process. The project coordinator was a city employee who initially devoted only part of her day to ETV, but the job quickly became a full-time responsibility. The project coordinator performed these tasks:

(1) prepare a newsletter to keep all theme group members informed about their respective progress;
(2) attend theme group meetings;
(3) cover for technical staff;
(4) prepare the budget for ETV;
(5) organize special events;
(6) supervise and assist city staff involved with ETV in general; and
(7) fix any problems associated with the mechanics of the planning process.

Special Events

Numerous special events were scheduled during the two-year process, such as workshops, lectures by consultants, tours, receptions, a retreat, and a conference. Several of the most significant special events are described below.

(1) The "kick-off" event was scheduled for March 28 and 29, 1988. Neal Peirce, a nationally known public affairs columnist, was hired to speak about other communities' planning experiences, and to comment on Rock Hill's approach. Workshops were held during the "kick-off" event in order to prepare the theme group members for their work.[13]

(2) Numerous consultants were hired to speak to the various theme groups. Michael Gallis, a professor of architecture at UNC-Charlotte, presented research on the nature of Rock Hill's position in the Charlotte MSA at the "kick-off" event, and later spoke about historic preservation and the importance of public art at theme group meetings.[14] David Schneider, a historic preservation consultant based in Charleston, South Carolina, talked to the Historic City theme group about research his firm had recently completed on the historic structures in Rock Hill.[15] Dianne

Abbey Lewis, director of Charleston's Office of Cultural Affairs, spoke to the Cultural City theme group about Charleston's experiences in using the arts to promote community development.[16] Charles Fink, a consultant on the development of greenways, spoke to the Garden City theme group about the creation of parks and walking, jogging and bicycling trails as a means of preserving open space and enhancing recreation opportunities in the city.[17] Robert Long, a theater-design consultant based in New York, discussed the size of a theater a community like Rock Hill could support with the Cultural City theme group.[18] Michael Verruto, a Charlotte based consultant who worked with Michael Gallis, discussed business trends in the Charlotte MSA with the Business City theme group.[19]

In addition to these "outside" consultants, several professionals from Rock Hill made formal presentations to various theme groups. A representative of Winthrop College, York Tech, Clinton College and Rock Hill School District No. 3 each spoke to the Education City theme group about their institutions.[20] Landscape-architect Duane Christopher presented a plan he had developed for the downtown to the Garden City theme group.[21] Dr. Bennett Lentczner, Dean of the School of Visual and Performing Arts at Winthrop College, met with the Cultural City theme group. He discussed the need for a partnership between Winthrop College and the city in order to create a hospitable environment for artists in the community.[22]

(3) Theme groups used several tours or site visits. The Garden City theme group traveled to Charlotte to tour the McAlpine Greenway.[23] The Historic City theme group arranged a tour of Salisbury, North Carolina's historic district.[24] The Functional City theme group toured the central Rock Hill area in order to assess roads, land-use patterns, intersections and utility wiring.[25] The Cultural City theme group toured Rock Hill by bus in order to have City Manager Lanford describe the possible changes in the city's appearance that could be made with the use of public art.[26]

(4) Opportunities to celebrate and to be entertained were also part of ETV. For example, after Neal Peirce's evening presentation on March 28, 1988, the Chamber of Commerce sponsored a reception. Also during the series of workshops on March 29, 1988, a luncheon for all the participants was scheduled.

(5) The members of the governing bodies of the seven sponsoring institutions and the co-chairpersons of each theme group were invited to attend a retreat in May 1989 in Myrtle Beach,SC.[27] The purpose of the retreat was to explain the details of the plan produced by the theme groups, consultants and staff to the leaders of these seven key institutions.

Their institutional endorsement was needed in order to facilitate the implementation of the ten-year plan. Part of the design of ETV included having the seven sponsoring institutions pass a resolution officially endorsing the plan and promising to do their share to make it a reality. The retreat format allowed the leaders to focus their attention on the ETV plan without having to consider their normal responsibilities back in Rock Hill.

(6) On September 26, 1989 the City of Rock Hill presented its planning process and the plan itself at a regional conference on creating a common vision for the Charlotte MSA.[28] Although Rock Hill civic leaders viewed the other *ring cities* in the metropolitan area as rivals for citizens and businesses, they decided that the better these cities were planned, the more attractive the entire region would be as a place to live and to locate new businesses.

Charettes

City Manager Lanford believed that creative solutions to problems often were found when people were brought together at a single location t o w ork i ntensely f or a s hort p eriod o f t ime. The chance to concentrate on the task and not be distracted by the routines of everyday work and living can be the catalyst people need to develop new ideas. He used to the French term, *charette*, which literally means "small handcart," to describe this intense approach he wanted the theme groups and staff to use. The explanation presented to the theme group participants in their handbook is as follows:

> The term *charette* comes from the Ecole des Arts in Paris, where art and architecture students used small handcarts (*charettes*) to rush their work to their assigned critics. Often the students would be drawing away while the carts were moving, giving the word the meaning of a last minute burst of activity to meet the deadline -- a usage common in architects' offices. In turn, architects like to use the term to describe what they are doing: going to a place to look at a specific problem and offering a solution in a very short period of time.[29]

City Manager Lanford hoped to have these intense work sessions and all other meetings of the theme groups take place at a central location. The facility ideally would be large enough to allow all theme groups to meet, perhaps simultaneously, and leave all of their work setup at their respective workstations. Although some cities may have had difficulty finding such a facility, especially one that was free, Rock Hill was able to secure one with relative ease.

Through Mayor Rhea's initiative, the city was able to contact the Belk Brothers Corporation of Charlotte, a major retail department store chain, in order to obtain use of the company's empty store in the TownCenter Mall. The company agreed to donate the store to the city. In addition, Winthrop College, York Tech, the Chamber of Commerce and Springs Industry donated furniture and equipment.[30]

The significance of using the Belk building was not lost on the sponsors of ETV. In 1977 Rock Hill became one of the hundreds of cities around the nation attempting to save their retail center in the downtown area by covering part of Main Street in order to create a mall.[31] Richard Francavilglia explains the logic cities followed in the 1970s: "Main Streets were closed to traffic in the hope that a pedestrian environment would improve retailing downtown (that is increase the number of people), and Main Street would thus be able to directly compete with shopping centers that were drawing away its trade."[32] Although successful at first, by the mid-1980s Rock Hill's TownCenter Mall began losing stores, such as the Belks' Budget Fair Store. The Mall had become part of the problem in the downtown area, and the debate over what to do about the mall divided the community. The question simply put: Should Rock Hill do what other cities with failed malls on Main Street have done and remove the roof and open-up the streets to cars and pedestrians? By using the Belk building as the main work site in the planning process, the city not only could use the *charette* approach, but also build on the symbolic quality of the particular location. Officials believed bringing citizens from all parts of the city to the downtown area, especially to the troubled TownCenter Mall, might help them recognize the need to create a vision for a new Rock Hill, an inspirational vision that would guide the redevelopment of the central core of the city.

In the Theme Group Handbook provided to each theme group member, the linkage of the *charette* approach and the Belk building was clearly stated:

> This is what each theme group will be doing over the
> course of the planning year. Instead of using handcarts,
> the downtown Belk's building has been selected as a

central location for all theme groups to meet and work on their plan/solution. This will allow the theme groups to visually display their work. The facility will be open to the public in order to inform the community of each theme group's progress and to provide the citizens with an opportunity to make comments.[33]

Models

Developing visual representations of the plans was a key task performed by the city graphics staff and by consultants, especially the Morgan-Adams Group of Charlotte. Charts, physical models, and computer-generated pictures were created in order to help the theme group members, community leaders, and the general public obtain a clear view and deeper appreciation of the vision of a new Rock Hill.

Charts listing the goal areas and the specific recommendations of each theme group were displayed at their respective workstations. The recommendations were listed by the year in which they were to be implemented. In order to reinforce the idea that the plan was a "living" plan that could be adjusted to meet the realities present in any one of the 10 years leading up to the year 2000, the recommendations were printed on removable tags. The theme groups could move one project from 1992 to 1994 if they thought the earlier date was not appropriate.

After the co-chairs of each theme group had reported their recommendations to the steering committee in October 1988, physical models of the downtown area and of the Gateway Plaza Project on the Dave Lyle Boulevard, which was the main product of Rock Hill's public art program, were constructed. The scale models were first presented at the Myrtle Beach retreat to the members of the governing boards of the seven sponsoring institutions and other people attending the event. The models were brought back to Rock Hill and placed in the Belk building for review by the theme group members, the downtown merchants and the general public.

In March 1990, the Morgan-Adams Group produced computer-generated images to illustrate how the plans in ETV would alter Rock Hill.[34] Color photographs of the various parts of the downtown area were scanned and digitalized by computer. The photographs were altered in order to reflect the possible changes that would occur if the plans were implemented.

The General Public

The general public participated in the process through three basic ways. First, city officials, steering committee members, city staff and the editors of the two newspapers in Rock Hill issued numerous calls for more citizen involvement in the process, especially as a theme group member. According to the Mayor Rhea, the "door was always open" to any citizen who wanted to contribute. Second, in August 1988 while the theme groups were meeting, two page *ideas forms* were placed at several locations around the city. The general public was invited to comment on the how the city could: (1) improve the cultural environment, the education system, the infrastructure, the green spaces and the city's image in the metropolitan area; (2) promote economic development; and (3) preserve the city's history.[35] Third, the general public was invited to tour the Belk building from July through September 1989 in order to see the models and review the details of the final plan. Those citizens who wanted to comment could write their views in a log placed at the Belk building. Over 700 hundred citizens went on the tour.

The Timetable

ETV began officially in January 1988. The steering committee completed its preliminary work by March 1988. The kick-off event was held over March 28-29, 1988. The theme groups began meeting in April and worked until October, seven months, to complete their plans. In October the co-chairs of each theme group presented their recommendations to the steering committee. From November 1988 to May 1989, the city staff and consultants worked on the various plans. Their job was to produce a single, coherent plan using the ideas offered by the theme groups. The plan was first revealed at the Myrtle Beach retreat on May 12, 1989. On July 5, the theme group participants were invited to see the models and the plan displayed at the Belk building. The downtown merchants and property owners were invited to see the plan on July 6. Between July 12 and September 30, the Belk building was opened to the general public. After September 30, 1989, the Belk building opened only for individuals or groups requesting a tour. The seven sponsoring institutions passed resolutions endorsing the plan between May and July 1989 (see Figure 2.1). In those resolutions, each sponsor promised "the projects and goals of the Central Rock Hill Plan (i.e., ETV) will be incorporated into the future planning and budget activities" of their institution. On September 26, 1989, Rock Hill presented its planning process and final plan at the regional conference in Charlotte. The implementation of the plan began officially in January 1990.

Figure 2.1 ETV Endorsement Resolution: City Version

A RESOLUTION TO ENDORSE THE
CENTRAL ROCK HILL PLAN
CITY COUNCIL OF ROCK HILL

BE IT RESOLVED by the City Council of Rock Hill, SC in a meeting duly assembled, that:

WHEREAS, the City of Rock Hill, Rock Hill Area Chamber of Commerce, the Rock Hill Economic Development Corporation, Rock Hill School District Number 3, Winthrop College, York County and York Technical College formed a planning coalition called the Central Rock Hill Plan Steering Committee; and

WHEREAS, the Steering Committee solicited the ideas of the citizens of Rock Hill to develop a vision for the community from the following theme perspectives: Historical City, Educational City, Garden City, Functional City, Business City and Cultural City; and

WHEREAS, on October 19, 1988, after nine months of study, the citizen advisory groups submitted to the Steering Committee their recommendations and goals for Rock Hill in the year 2000; and

WHEREAS, these recommendations and goals have been transformed into a plan for the development of the Central Rock Hill area; and

WHEREAS, ON May 12, 1989, in a joint meeting, this plan was presented to the Governing Bodies of the Steering Committee and to the Co-chairpersons of each theme group; and

WHEREAS, this plan promotes planned growth, fosters quality economic development, provides for amenities that will improve quality of life, and creates a new image for Rock Hill as it enters the Twenty-first

(continued)

Figure 2.1 Continued

Century; and

WHEREAS, cooperation between the seven institutions represented on the Steering Committee is essential for realizing the goals of the plan and the aspirations of each individual institution;

NOW THEREFORE, the City Council of Rock Hill, SC does hereby resolve and declare that:

1. The recitals hereof are true and correct.
2. It endorses the vision for Rock Hill contained in the Central Rock Hill Plan.
3. The implementation of the Rock Hill Plan will benefit the City Council, and the entire community of Rock Hill and York County.
4. The projects and goals of the Central Rock Hill Plan will be incorporated into the future planning and budget activities of the City Council.
5. The Steering Committee shall continue to meet and shall keep the respective Governing Bodies informed on the plan implementation.
6. That a biennial conference will be held by the Governing Bodies of the Central Rock Hill Plan to review and revise the plan.
7. That regular citizen involvement should continue throughout the implementation of the Central Rock Hill Plan.

DONE AND RATIFIED on this 22ⁿᵈ day of May, 1989

_____
Elizabeth D. Rhea, Mayor

_____
Gerald E. Shapiro, Municipal Clerk

The city intended to follow a flexible schedule for implementing the plan and to remain open to needed changes in the details of the plan. In fact changes in the plan occurred in 1990, the first year of implementation. This flexible approach was based on the idea that ETV should be a "living" plan. City Manager Lanford, Mayor Rhea and other officials believed the key to success was to keep in mind the vision, the definition of the city's identity, while adjustments would be made in the details of the plan over time.

In addition, the steering committee and theme groups planned to meet periodically during the ten year process in order to see how much had been accomplished, how much remained to be done, and what needed to be changed. This design creatively altered the nature of the policymaking process in Rock Hill by institutionalizing a strategic planning technique that included a large number of the city's most influential citizens. Any discussion of city policy in the future invariably would involve a number of citizens who would be aware of the city's plan and who would want to discuss the proposals in light of the plan.

Summary

Rock Hill's ETV was an innovative application of the strategic planning technique. This description of the process reveals the unique character of Rock Hill's effort. The use of multiple sponsors, planning staff, theme groups, workshops, consultants, site visits, a central location, *charettes*, models and the idea of a "living" plan are all valuable features that could be used with success in other communities. This process produced a plan that would change Rock Hill in significant ways, if fully implemented. The emphasis on public art, historic preservation, gardens, greenways, downtown office development and cultural events produced an inspiring effort to transform the city's 1970s-early-1980s identity as an *old textile-city in decline* into a 1990s-new century identity as a *Southern urban village on the leading edge of Charlotte.*

Chapter 3

Lessons from the Planning Process: 1987-1989

The role of leadership in collaboration is to engage others by designing constructive processes for working together, convene appropriate stakeholders, and facilitate and sustain their interaction.
- David D. Chrislip and Carl E. Larson

Community-wide strategic planning is difficult to do, but there are successful efforts that can serve as role models for other cities.[1] Rock Hill is one of those cities. Rock Hill's success in completing the process can encourage other medium-size cities to take the risks and invest the resources needed to use this new tool. What can be learned from the Rock Hill experience using community-wide strategic planning? Why was ETV successful? Can ETV's features be applied in other cities? Using these basic questions to evaluate ETV offers nine important lessons (see Appendix A for a description of the research design for stage one).

Lesson 1: Rely on Strong, Stable, Public Leadership

For strategic planning to succeed, Bryson suggests "there is no substitute for leadership."[2] The departure of the chief sponsor and champion can be fatal.[3] In contrast, the persistence of a popular leader can make community-wide strategic planning successful.[4] Although there are pros and cons to having the city provide the leading role,[5] it was a clear advantage in Rock Hill's case to have city officials initiate and sponsor the community-wide strategic planning effort. Indeed, 27 percent of the 51 theme group participants responding to my survey in 1990 cited the city's leadership as the most impressive feature of ETV.

The presence of two strong executive leaders was a key reason why ETV succeeded. City Manager Lanford and Mayor Rhea were the key process sponsors and champions. Community leaders described them as "visionaries or dreamers." Their working relationship was built on mutual respect. Rhea admired Lanford's planning skill and ability to think creatively about the city's future. Lanford admired Rhea's public relations skills, her full-time dedication to the job, and her strong love for Rock Hill. Their teamwork combined Rhea's skills as a facilitative-type leader with Lanford's planning expertise.[6] As one respondent suggested, "the looking ahead part of ETV came from Joe Lanford, but the getting-everyone-involved part was all Betty Jo."

Lesson 2: Use Sufficient Public Resources

Community-wide strategic planning can be costly, often requiring several hundred thousand dollars.[7] Donna Sorkin, Nancy Ferris and James Hudak suggest "short-cut approaches to strategic planning are likely to fall short of the mark."[8] Although total budget figures on ETV's cost do not exist, estimates based on some of the main components paid for by the city, including consultant fees, printing, travel, meals, model construction, basic office supplies, and staff time indicate ETV cost the city well over $200,000. Omitted from this total is the value of the time spent by volunteers and the value of office furniture and meeting space provided by other sponsors. Clearly, Rock Hill did not try to take a short-cut approach.

Lesson 3: Involve Key Institutions

Advocates of community-wide strategic planning recommend forming a coalition of major stakeholders to support the process.[9] Rock Hill's ETV met these concerns by securing the sponsorship of seven community institutions with the resources needed to implement a ten-year plan, involving citizens in the theme groups who were members and leaders in over 36 community organizations (see Table 3.1), and working well with the local newspapers. Of the 86 participants in my 1990 research, 17 percent cited this unprecedented level of institutional cooperation as one of ETV's most impressive features.

Table 3.1 Community Organizations Represented in ETV

Rotary Club	United Way Board
RH Country Club	United Arts Fund Committee
Optimist Club	Newcomers Club
Junior Women's Club	"Come See Me" Festival Board
Leroy Springs Art Society	Fine Arts Association
YMCA	Mid-Town Preservation Association
Chamber of Commerce	Junior Welfare League
Kiwanis	Museum of York County Board
RH Arts Council	Winthrop College Board of Visitors
RH Little Theater	York Tech Foundation
Sierra Club	Lions Club
American Red Cross	RH School District Foundation
Friends of the Library	Central City Optimist Club
NAACP	RH Human Rights Council
League of Women Voters	Delta Kappa Gamma
Sister Help	RH MultiCultural Art Committee
AAUW	Friends of Historic Brattonsville
YC Genealogical & Historical Society	East Town Neighborhood Association

Notes: RH = Rock Hill; YC = York County; Memberships reported by survey respondents only.

Lesson 4: Find Strong Process Champions

Process champions are important to the successful completion of strategic planning efforts.[10] Sorkin, Ferris and Hudak suggest choosing task force chairs carefully because "these individuals will be given considerable responsibility for producing analyses whose quality is crucial to the success of the overall effort."[11] John Bryson and William Roering found in their cases that the process champions "were always the team leader or co-leader."[12] ETV received strong leadership from not only the co-chairs of the theme groups but also from the project coordinator.

Participants in my 1990 research were asked to identify individuals who emerged as leaders and champions of the process. Of the 124 citizens serving on the theme groups, 19 were identified as process champions. The co-chairs of the Business City, Functional City, and Cultural City theme groups, as well as one of the chairs of the Garden City and Historic City theme groups, received the most nominations as process champions from their co-workers. No one was identified as a champion on the Education City theme group, which helps to explain why it received mixed reviews for its performance from its members and other observers.

Whereas process champions are needed, Bryson and Roering suggest "even process champions . . . could fall into gumption traps."[13] In some cities, outside consultants act "as cheerleaders for the champions, helping to keep their spirits up and encouraging them to push the process along".[14] In Rock Hill, the project coordinator, Annie Porter, became the cheerleader of the champions, as well as a process champion par excellence. ETV participants praised her performance. They described her as "the glue that held the process together," "the close-to-the-details person," and the person who "did everything at all levels." When asked to rate her performance from (1) poor to (5) excellent, the 51 theme-group respondents awarded her a 4.6.

Lesson 5: Use Consultants as Educators

Consultants can play a key role in community-wide strategic planning.[15] Bryson suggests often "organizations and communities need some consultation, facilitation, and education from outsiders."[16] City Manager Lanford's planning expertise and his talented staff allowed Rock Hill to eschew using consultants for designing and implementing the process. Instead, Rock Hill used outside consultants primarily as community educators.

Theme groups heard expert presentations on historic preservation, urban development, public art, theater design, greenways (open space) development, and landscape design.[17] The choice of topics reflects the influence of the planning staff guiding the theme group discussions over a seven-month period. By using consultants as educators, Rock Hill avoided a consultant-dominated process, a pitfall for many strategic planning efforts.[18]

Lesson 6: Use a Creative Work Process in a Highly Symbolic Setting

Creative decisions emerge from processes best described as intuitive, ambiguous, messy, fluid, risky, and open.[19] Bringing people together to brainstorm is a major part of the creative process in strategic planning intended to generate creative ideas and strategies to accomplish them.[20] ETV's design reflected this creative approach.

Lanford used *charettes* as a method to nurture creative thinking. He encouraged participants to suspend their concerns for being practical and cost-conscious.[21] Lanford wanted to avoid cost estimates, because "it is impossible to base a good plan on costs. We wanted people to concentrate on dreaming."[22] The *charettes* were held at the Belk building. This empty retail department store was a main symbol of the downtown's decline, so by using it in ETV, Lanford hoped it would be a symbol to motivate participants to plan Rock Hill's future.

Did the Belk building have the desired impact? When asked to rate the importance of this facility to ETV's success on a scale from (1) not important to (4) very important, 62 percent of the 86 participants in my 1990 research thought it was important or very important. And overall, it received a 2.9 mean rating ($n=69$, 17 don't know responses were excluded). A business leader offered a typical comment suggesting, "It was very important. We could display everything. We could have plenty of meetings and we could accommodate hundreds of people. The main advantage was that all groups could see what others were doing, so leaving everything posted was great."

Lesson 7: Visualize Changes

Support for the product of strategic planning relates to the extent to which the people affected by the plan can visualize how it will change their current condition.[23] Producing an inspirational written statement describing the future was the conventional approach.[24] Rock Hill chose to downplay the idea of a written plan. As Lanford explained, "we didn't set out to make a spiral bound plan."[25] Instead, numerous charts, physical models, and computer-generated pictures helped the participants and citizens visualize the new Rock Hill.

The city graphics staff and consultants developed these visual aids. Charts listing the goal areas and the specific recommendations of each theme group were displayed at their respective workstations in the Belk building. Near the end of the process, consultants built physical models of the downtown area and of the Gateway Plaza Project on Dave Lyle Boulevard as a way to help visualize the plan. In March 1990, the Morgan-Adams Group produced computer-generated images to illustrate how the plan would alter Rock Hill.[26] Lanford presented these pictures to the city council at a televised meeting, and some of them were printed along with news articles in *The Herald*.

Lesson 8: Secure Broad-Based Citizen Participation

Community-wide strategic planning depends upon extensive citizen participation in order to develop ideas, build a consensus, and secure the resources to implement the plan.[27] There are many mechanisms available to involve the public, such as task forces, public hearings/ forums, and surveys.[28] Rock Hill used a task force approach. Each task force (i.e., theme group) held public meetings and used a variety of information gathering tools, such as site visits, lectures, and surveys.

There are also several ways to select citizen participants to serve on task forces, including nomination by key community organizations, appointment by sponsoring institutions, election, and open invitation.[29] Rock Hill issued an open invitation combined with a specific invitation to citizens nominated by ETV leaders. Rhea, Lanford, and other members of the steering committee and city government prepared the initial invitation list. They used an informal, brainstorming approach to identify potential participants. One official described the process as follows: "We sat around the table and tried to identify the best and the brightest people who we knew had a civic spirit about them. We wanted people who would work and dedicate themselves to the task, and who would provide a broad representation of the city. We wanted to have women, minorities, geographic areas, and denominational groups represented in the process."

Once the groups were formed, ETV staff encouraged the membership of each group to invite other citizens to join them, especially from the African-American community. In addition, Rhea, Lanford, Porter, city council members, steering committee members, and the editor of *The Herald*, issued public calls for citizen involvement throughout the process.

ETV leaders clearly had two conceptions of representation in mind as they nominated and discussed candidates, descriptive and substantive.[30] First, they wanted to invite a descriptively representative group of civic leaders, especially regarding race and gender. Second, their preference for civic leaders who shared a general interest in making Rock Hill a better place to live and who had particular expertise in one of the six theme areas, reveals a substantive element. ETV leaders wanted to attract people who held what Edward Banfield and James Q. Wilson called a "public-regarding ethos."[31] Therefore, people perceived to be too narrow (i.e., pushing neighborhood projects) or too critical of city government were not initially invited. However, no one was excluded if they wanted to participate.

Did the ETV leaders successfully attract a descriptively representative group of citizens to work on the theme groups? Data on political party affiliation, organizational membership, gender, race, occupation, and election ward indicate only partial success.

Data on political party affiliation and organizational memberships are available only for the 51 survey respondents. Based on my 1990 survey data, ETV leaders successfully attracted citizens with varied partisan perspectives (see Table 3.2). ETV leaders also involved citizens with a record of civic involvement. About 57 percent of the survey

Table 3.2 Theme Group Participants by Political Party

Group	Dem	Rep	Ind	Missing
Business (n = 10)	2 (20)	3 (30)	2 (20)	3 (30)
Garden (n = 6)	1 (17)	3 (50)	2 (33)	0 (0)
Historic (n= 11)	6 (55)	1 (9)	1 (9)	3 (27)
Functional (n = 8)	6 (75)	1 (12)	1 (12)	0 (0)
Educational (n = 4)	2 (50)	2 (50)	0 (0)	0 (0)
Cultural (n = 12)	1 (8)	5 (42)	2 (17)	4 (33)
Total (N = 51)	18 (35)	15 (29)	8 (16)	10 (20)

Notes: Data from survey respondents only. The numbers is parentheses are percentages. The percentages are calculated across rows. Rows that do not add up to 100 percent are due to rounding.

respondents indicated they had held appointed office in Rock Hill, and 59 percent indicated they belonged to more than three community organizations.

The data on gender in Table 3.3, on race in Table 3.4 and on occupations in Table 3.5 are complete for all 124 ETV participants. The data indicate the typical ETV participant was male, white, and employed as a professional or business manager.   About 28 percent of the participants were women who served mainly on the Garden City, Historic City, and Cultural City theme groups. The African-American community, which was one-third of Rock Hill's population, was underrepresented in ETV, accounting for only 12 percent of the invited participants. Blue-collar and service-worker occupations also were underrepresented. While these occupations counted for well over 50 percent of the work force,[32] none of the theme groups had more than one person with a blue-collar or service-worker occupation.

Table 3.3 Theme Group Participants by Gender

Group	Male	Female
Business (n = 20)	17 (85)	3 (15)
Garden (n = 21)	15 (71)	6 (29)
Historic (n = 20)	12 (60)	8 (40)
Functional (n = 20)	18 (90)	2 (10)
Educational (n = 18)	15 (83)	3 (17)
Cultural (n= 25)	12 (48)	13 (52)
Total (N = 124)	89 (72)	35 (28)

Notes: The numbers in parentheses are percentages.
The percentages are calculated across rows.

The data in Table 3.6 on geographic representation must be interpreted cautiously. Not only are data missing for 24 percent of the 124 citizens, but the six wards were created in 1989, almost two years after ETV began, so the individuals preparing the invitation list worked with a different electoral map. With this in mind, the data indicate 66 percent of the citizens lived in wards two, four, five, and six. The low rate of participation from wards one (4 percent) and three (4 percent) reflected the under-representation of African-Americans and blue-collar workers.

Table 3.4 Theme Group Participants by Race

Group	White	Black	Asian
Business (n = 20)	19 (95)	1 (5)	0 (0)
Garden (n = 21)	18 (86)	3 (14)	0 (0)
Historic (n = 20)	18 (90)	2 (10)	0 (0)
Functional (n = 20)	17 (85)	3 (15)	0 (0)
Educational (n = 18)	13 (72)	5 (28)	0 (0)
Cultural (n= 25)	21 (84)	1 (4)	3 (12)
Total (N = 124)	106 (85)	15 (12)	3 (3)

Notes: The numbers in parentheses are percentages.
The percentages are calculated across rows.

The survey and interviews produced two contrasting perspectives on this participation pattern. First, over 40 percent of the 86 respondents cited extensive public involvement as ETV's most impressive feature. They praised ETV for the unprecedented willingness of Rock Hill's many organizations and institutions to work together. They praised ETV participants for working hard (based on survey data, each theme group member worked an average of 3.5 hours per week and missed an average of only 2.5 meetings over seven months). In contrast, 21 percent of the 86 respondents, including four members of the steering committee, cited the lack of African-American participation as the most important problem with the ETV process.

ETV leaders who helped identify and invite citizens were among the 40 percent who praised public involvement. ETV leaders expressed frustration and disappointment with their inability to convince more African-American leaders to get involved, but ETV leaders defended their approach. One ETV leader responded, "We begged people to join. We advertised. It was their own fault. Anybody could have walked down to the Belk building to take part. It's a plan for the whole community –

Table 3.5 Theme Group Participants by Occupation

Group	Gov't	Bus	Prof	Civic	Other
Business (n = 20)	1 (5)	13 (65)	6 (30)	0 (0)	0 (0)
Garden (n = 21)	1 (5)	6 (29)	11 (52)	3 (14)	0 (0)
Historic (n = 20)	1 (5)	4 (20)	11 (55)	3 (15)	1 (5)
Functional (n = 20)	2 (10)	7 (35)	9 (45)	1 (5)	1 (5)
Educational (n = 18)	1 (6)	7 (39)	10 (55)	0 (0)	0 (0)
Cultural (n = 25)	6 (24)	6 (24)	10 (40)	3 (12)	0 (0)
Total (N = 124)	12 (10)	43 (35)	57 (46)	10 (8)	2 (1)

Notes: The numbers in parentheses are percentages. All percentages are calculated across rows. Government occupations are city employee, nonprofit agency director, and school administrator. Business occupations are bank manager, corporate executive, retail shop owner, and sales manager. Professional occupations are lawyer, teacher, physician, minister, architect, and professor. Civic occupations are homemakers who volunteer their time. Other occupations include construction employee, factory employee and restaurant service employee.

It's just a plan to guide the future. We invited all the churches, including the black ministers. It was an open process." If ETV leaders wanted extensive African-American participation, why were many African-American leaders absent? Interview responses pointed to two main problems with the method used to identify and invite ETV participants.

First, the emphasis on finding people who would help create a vision not linked to neighborhood concerns discouraged community leaders who wanted to work on such problems. For example, some of the African-American citizens in the Crawford Road area who had helped produce a neighborhood plan in 1987 wanted to see the city begin to

Table 3.6 Theme Group Participants by Ward

Group	Ward 1	Ward 2	Ward 3	Ward 4	Ward 5	Ward 6	Non-Residents	Don't Know
Business (n=20)	0 (0)	5 (25)	0 (0)	4 (20)	3 (15)	2 (10)	0 (0)	6 (30)
Garden (n=21)	0 (0)	4 (19)	1 (5)	8 (38)	0 (0)	5 (24)	0 (0)	3 (14)
Historic (n=20)	2 (10)	1 (5)	2 (10)	1 (5)	5 (25)	5 (25)	1 (5)	3 (15)
Functional (n=20)	0 (0)	1 (5)	1 (5)	8 (40)	1 (5)	0 (0)	1 (5)	8 (40)
Educational (n=18)	3 (17)	1 (6)	1 (6)	4 (22)	4 (22)	2 (11)	0 (0)	3 (17)
Cultural (n=25)	0 (0)	5 (20)	0 (0)	4 (16)	4 (16)	4 (16)	1 (4)	7 (28)
Total (N = 124)	5 (4)	17 (14)	6 (5)	29 (23)	17 (14)	18 (15)	3 (2)	30 (24)

Notes: Numbers in parentheses are percentages. Percentages are calculated across rows. "Don't know" indicates the numbers of citizen participants who provided only a business address and did not otherwise indicate their ward.

implement the improvements recommended in that plan. Because ETV was not the appropriate forum for discussing the need for drainage improvements in neighborhoods, road repair, sidewalk construction, and housing rehabilitation, they concluded participating in ETV would not be a good use of their time. One individual captured this sentiment by suggesting "the first thing to do is get water out of my yard, some sidewalks built, some potholes fixed; then once these physical needs are met we can begin to think about culture, the arts, and so on."

Second, the lack of African-American participation in the preparation of the invitation list discouraged African-American leaders. Because they did not help prepare the initial invitation list, some of the African-American leaders perceived the invitations as token opportunities. One leader explained "what happened is traditional. Some people were identified as traditional leaders. 'I know so and so, lets call him.' The black community did not speak for themselves. So we perceived it as tokenism."

Another leader suggested, "If you want to get blacks involved don't rely on white organizers to set up meetings. The main reason they didn't want us is because we'll bring up the concerns of the poor people." A leader from the Crawford Road area suggested that "they could've gotten long-term residents from neighborhoods that had a stake in the black community, like Boyd Hill, Flint Hill, and Crawford Road."

These comments point to three changes that could produce a more representative process in heterogeneous communities like Rock Hill. First, the circle of leaders involved in preparing the invitation list and directing the development of an ETV-type process should be as diverse as the population. Second, including the major concerns directly affecting the quality of life in the low-income and African-American neighborhoods can increase participation. Third, building the capacity to be involved in a strategic planning effort can also help increase participation. As a first step in a planning process, some cities need to organize and train the participants and use preplanning workshops to work through emotional issues.[33]

Lesson 9: Use a Living Plan

A major advantage strategic planning has over traditional planning approaches is the emphasis on monitoring and updating the plan and process.[34] ETV incorporated this kind of flexible schedule. ETV leaders believed the key to success was to keep in mind the vision, the definition of the city's identity, while adjustments could be made in the details of the plan over time. Lanford designed ETV as a "living" plan, so "if everybody does a little bit each year according to the vision, then the plan will make a difference. If the plan is completed in five years, 10 years, or 15 years, OK. The key is moving in a direction."[35]

During the 1990s, the steering committee would be responsible for coordinating ETV's implementation and for revising the plan. The steering committee and theme groups planned to meet periodically during the ten-year process in order to see how much has been accomplished, how much remained to be done, and what needed to be changed.   City officials, especially Lanford, planned to lead those efforts.

In fact, changes were made in the first year of implementation in order to address the concerns of the African-American community. In July 1990, the City of Rock Hill joined with First Union National Bank to start and fund a Neighborhood Improvement Program.[36] The program targeted the low-income areas of the city in order to develop emerging leadership. Also in August 1990, Rock Hill prepared to spend Community Development Block Grant (CDBG) money received from the national government to establish a housing development corporation and to improve water, sewer, roads, and drainage services in the Porter Road and Crawford Road areas.[37] These changes mitigated the detrimental effects on consensus building caused by the method used to secure citizen participation and reflected Rock Hill's use of a "living" plan.

An Emergent Consensus in Rock Hill

The ETV process produced a plan that received widespread public approval. The governing boards of all seven sponsors passed resolutions endorsing the plan and pledging to implement their parts. Between July and November 1989, more than 700 citizens from over 70 different community organizations toured the Belk building in order to see the models and charts depicting the final plan. Over 97 percent of the 147 comments written in the comment log were positive. People described the plan as "excellent, great, super, impressive, very progressive, and most interesting."[38] Even critics who expressed concern about African-American participation liked ETV's product, especially after neighborhood improvements and housing were added.

In 1990 there was a renewed sense of community identity and a willingness to work together in Rock Hill. ETV clearly helped establish support for several major changes that expanded the pluralist regime's agenda to include middle-class progressive initiatives, such as:

(1) removing the roof of the TownCenter Mall;
(2) establishing a downtown arts and theater center;
(3) creating historic districts;
(4) establishing a greenway system;
(5) creating a civic square;
(6) purchasing public art (like the Gateway Plaza Project);
(7) improving neighborhood infrastructure; and
(8) spending public money to initiate redevelopment and build business parks.

People were optimistic that ETV's implementation would transform Rock Hill into a vibrant community with a unique identity in the Charlotte MSA.

Summary

This case study demonstrates the effectiveness of strategic planning as a tool for community-wide planning and collaborative problem solving. ETV used several standard features of a strategic planning process successfully: using sufficient resources, securing key sponsors, communicating through the media, using task forces, appointing co-chairs of task forces, hiring consultants, and monitoring and updating the plan. Rock Hill also created unique process features: *charettes*, a symbolic work setting, and developing visual plans instead of a written document. These standard and unique process features could be applied in other cities.

ETV also demonstrated the limitations of the invitation method of securing citizen participation. Even if the leaders issuing invitations reflect the diversity of the population, capacity-building and pre-planning workshops may be needed to prepare citizens for the strategic planning process. In addition, the range of interests and issues covered by the process should be broad enough to attract a cross-section of the community.

Finally, ETV demonstrated the importance of public leadership to a community-wide process. Although other cities may not need to have public officials with the facilitative, planning, and coordinating skills of Rock Hill's mayor, city manager, and project coordinator, their public officials at least need to promote the process and provide the financial and staff resources to support it. Ultimately, they need to be willing to respond constructively to criticism, adjusting the process and the plan to make both inclusive of varied community interests. Rock Hill's public leaders made this kind of commitment.

Chapter 4

Achieving the Vision: ETV Ten Years Later

Implementation often involves a whole new set of actors; therefore, considerable communication, education, and guidance may be necessary to get everyone "on board."

- Barbara C. Crosby

Gordon suggests "to fully appreciate the benefits of strategic planning, it is useful to recognize its nature: it is both a *process* and a *product*."[1] Clearly, cities derive benefits from doing a strategic plan as well as implementing a strategic plan, but ultimately a successful plan should alter the community in measurable ways. A review of the literature on public sector planning, collaborative decision-making, and governance theory suggests five significant results, including managing uncertainty by promoting learning, resolving conflict, involving citizens, producing tangible and intangible results, and establishing a governance network for the duration of the planning period. Did Rock Hill achieve these results after ten years? The evidence presented here suggests Rock Hill's leaders did achieve these results. They successfully implemented and updated ETV and by doing so altered the city in substantial and measurable ways (see the Appendix for a description of the research design for the stage two).

Managing Uncertainty

Advocates of public sector strategic planning identify the management of uncertainty about the future as one of the primary benefits of using this tool.[2] Uncertainty is managed through the initial strategic planning process by using professional expertise to help participants learn about their community and the forces affecting its future as they work to produce a plan, and through implementation by monitoring and revising the plan as conditions warrant. Sorkin, Ferris, and Hudak argue:

> . . . successful strategic planning requires continuing review of actual accomplishments in comparison with the plan . . . [and] periodic or continuous environmental scanning to assure that unforeseen developments do not sabotage the adopted plan or that emerging opportunities are not overlooked.[3]

Clearly assigning responsibility to monitor the plan's implementation to one of the sponsoring organizations, perhaps the organization that championed the process, will help insure the performance of this key task.[4] Key questions are: Was responsibility clearly assigned to a sponsoring organization?; Did the community monitor and revise the plan during the implementation process?; Did the initiative use expert knowledge to inform and educate?; Did the initiative foster learning among the participants?

Assigning Responsibility. As the main champions of the ETV planning process, city officials also accepted the responsibility to monitor the implementation of the plan. Mayor Betty Jo Rhea, who served from 1985 until she retired in 1998, and City Manager Joe Lanford, who served from 1979 until he retired in 1993, both are widely recognized by community leaders as the key leaders supporting ETV. Their successors, Mayor Doug Echols (1998 to present) and City Manager Russell Allen (1993 to 2001), also supported ETV-related projects and the use of strategic planning to address the city's future. These officials worked with the city council, the city-staffed RHEDC and its board of directors, and ETV's other sponsors to implement many projects. Throughout the 1990s, they used numerous formal and informal meetings with leaders of the sponsoring organizations and with other community leaders to monitor, revise, and build support for the plan.[5] Indeed through 1996 they used formal meetings of the steering committee to review ETV's implementation and encourage support for implementing projects.

Monitoring and Revising. Mid-way through the ten year implementation period, in October 1994, Mayor Rhea and City Manager Allen encouraged the steering committee to initiate a five year review of ETV's accomplishments and persuaded the committee to start a new community-wide strategic planning process to update the plan. After much discussion, the steering committee decided to change the name of the planning process from ETV to Empowering the Community (ETC) in order to reflect the new emphasis on neighborhood empowerment.[6] The steering committee also expanded to eight members in order to welcome the Catawba Indian Nation, which had recently settled its land dispute, as a sponsor (see Table 4.1).

The same six theme groups used in ETV were used in ETC. ETV theme group participants were invited to serve again, as well as were many other community leaders and the general public. Of the 176 ETC theme group participants, 26 had participated in ETV, which provided an important historical perspective to the discussions. After a kick-off event on April 27 and 28, 1995, theme groups met four times between May and September at different locations around the city. Each session lasted about two hours. City staff compiled the various recommendations during the Fall of 1995, and joined with theme group participants to present the Final Report on February 15, 1996 at a reception held at Winthrop University. The ETC planning phase officially ended on January 1, 1997, when a 16 page special insert entitled, "1997 Resolutions," appeared in *The Herald*. This publication reviewed ETV's accomplishments and called for citizens to support the implementation of ETC's ideas.

At the end of the ten-year implementation period, in November 1999, the RHEDC devoted its annual planning retreat to a retrospective on ETV and ETC. Leaders from all of ETV/ETC's sponsoring organizations were invited to the retreat and only representatives of the Catawba Indian Nation did not attend. The 50 leaders who attended the three-day event examined ETV plans and identified the projects that had been completed. They recognized that ETV had changed Rock Hill, and the sponsoring organizations, in ways called for in the plan they adopted in 1989. Although they generally thought ETC had added less value to ETV than they had hoped, in part due to the limited number of new projects added to the ones carried over from ETV, they were proud of the neighborhood empowerment initiative (see below). But the purpose of the retreat was more than an opportunity to look back at ETV/ETC. The leaders discussed ways to re-kindle the motivation to work together in order to build on their success. And they discussed whether another community-wide strategic planning effort would serve the community as ETV/ETC had done.

Table 4.1 ETC Steering Committee Members

Institution	Representatives
City of Rock Hill	Elizabeth D. Rhea, Mayor J. Russell Allen, City Manager Osbey Roddey, City Council
Rock Hill School District #3	Jane Peeples, Chair of School Board Ted Melton, Retired School Board Phillip McDaniel, Superintendent
Rock Hill Area Chamber of Commerce	Buzz Elliot, President Barre Mitchell Bayles Mack
RHEDC	David Vipperman, Chairman Clarence Hornsby, Vice Chairman Stephen Turner, Planning Consultant
York Technical College	J. Hank Owen, Chairman Dennis Merrell, President Joann Burt
Winthrop College	Anthony DiGiorgio, President Becky McMillan, Vice President Robert L. Thompson, Chair, Board of Trustees
York County	Carl Gullick, Council Chairman Clay Killian, County Manager
Catawba Indian Nation	Gilbert Blue, Chief Buck George, Assistant Chief Wanda Warren, Tribal Administrator

Using Expertise. During the ETV planning process in the late 1980s, Rock Hill called upon numerous experts to inform and educate the theme group participants and the public (see Chapters 2 and 3). Throughout the 1990s, Rock Hill continued to call on experts to provide information on some of the ETV-related projects being implemented. City officials contracted with Broach, Mijeski & Associates to do public opinion surveys to determine support for projects, such as city beautification, renovating the downtown business district by removing the roof of TownCenter Mall in order to open-up Main Street, and business park development.[7] The Rock Hill Chamber of Commerce also had Broach, Mijeski & Associates survey public opinion to determine support for downtown revitalization.[8] City officials also welcomed the advice of business leaders who had formed task forces to study city financial practices. One example of a task force is Citizens For Rock Hill's Future, which was a group formed in 1996 to review the city's management of the electric utility fund.[9] And during ETC, participants heard from consultants and various speakers on 21st Century trends, the basics of strategic planning, consensus-building techniques, historic preservation, landscape design, economic development trends affecting Rock Hill, how greenway systems can help preserve a community's identity, and the culture of the Catawba Indian Nation.

    Fostering Learning. The theme group participants' self-assessments of their learning provide a direct test of how well ETV/ETC fostered learning. The data in Table 4.2 for statements one and two indicate ETV/ETC helped to educate theme group participants about their community. The mean response for each question is above the 2.5 mid-point on the four-point scale suggesting participants thought they had learned.[10] Indeed, over 82 percent of the theme group participants "agreed" or "strongly agreed" that they had learned of more opportunities to work with other people and their organizations, and had learned a lot about Rock Hill's problems and solutions to those problems. Furthermore, the data in Table 4.3 indicate the majority of participants involved in ETV only, in ETC only, and in both initiatives "agreed" or "strongly agreed" with these statements.

Resolving Conflict

    Community-wide strategic planning is a form of collaborative decision-making.[11] Donald Chrislip and Carl Larson define collaboration as a "mutually beneficial relationship between two or more parties who work toward common goals by sharing responsibility, authority, and accountability for achieving results."[12] Because community-wide strategic planning is a form of collaboration, differences over goals and means that surface are resolved preferably through consensus building as a tool in traditional comprehensive planning.[13] But other forms of conflict resolution also are appropriate, perhaps even necessary, including coalition-building via compromise and accommodation.[14] If the planning

Table 4.2 Theme Group Participants' Views of Their Experiences in ETV and/or ETC

Statement (name)	Mean (n)	% ≥ 3
1. I learned of more opportunities to work with other people and their organizations to promote our mutual interests in addition to the community's more general interest. (Opportunity)	2.91 (112)	80.4
2. I learned a lot about Rock Hill's problems and alternative solutions to those problems. (Learn)	3.06 (112)	83.9
3. I developed a more effective working relationship with Rock Hill's active citizens, especially the business, civic, neighborhood, and political leaders. (Relations)	3.03 (113)	82.3
4. I became more willing to contribute my time, effort, and other resources to help Rock Hill become a better place in which to live and work. (Willing)	3.06 (113)	84.1
5. The citizens who participated in ETV and ETC were able to set aside their vested interests to achieve the common goal of improving Rock Hill. (Common)	2.91 (111)	80.2
6. I was inspired by ETV and ETC to do my part to make the plans a reality. (Inspired)	2.97 (110)	80.9
7. I developed a more positive view of Rock Hill's citizens, especially the business, civic, neighborhood, and political leaders. (View)	3.04 (113)	83.2

(continued)

Table 4.2 Continued

Statement (name)	Mean (n)	% ≥ 3
8. The openness and credibility of Rock Hill's community-wide strategic planning initiatives helped me set aside doubts and skepticism about them. (Credibility)	2.65 (108)	63.9
9. I developed a greater level of trust in Rock Hill's citizens, especially in the city's political leaders, to be open to my ideas and my interests. (Trust)	2.73 (111)	62.3
10. Those citizens in positions of power or authority have been willing to go along with many of the most important recommendations in ETV and ETC. (Go Along)	2.86 (109)	78.0

process is used skillfully, then Sorkin, Ferris, and Hudak believe "there should be broad consensus about what the issues are, how the external environment will affect the community, and what the strengths and weaknesses are. . . [and] new coalitions of business, government, and community members will have been formed with a commitment to specific strategies."[15] Key questions are: Did the initiative foster stronger working relationships among the participants?; Were participants more willing to contribute their time, effort, and other resources to help implement the plan?; Were participants able to set aside their vested interests to help achieve common goals?; Were participants inspired?; and Did the initiative organize interests to form a stable constituency to support the plan?

Relationships, Willingness, Common Goals, Inspiration. The data reported in Table 4.2 for statements three, four, five and six indicate the mean responses to each question are greater than 2.5 and over 80 percent of the respondents "agreed" or "strongly agreed" with each statement. They believed by participating on a theme group they "developed a more effective working relationship with Rock Hill's active citizens. . ."; they "became more willing to contribute their time, effort, and other resources to help Rock Hill. . ."; that other citizens "who participated in ETV and ETC were able to set aside their vested interests . . .;" and they were "inspired by ETV and ETC . . . ." In addition, the data in Table 4.3 indicate the majority of participants involved in ETV only, in ETC only, and in both initiatives "agreed" or "strongly agreed" with these statements.

Table 4.3 Theme Group Participants Views of their Experiences by Initiative (Percent "agree" or "strongly agree" reported)

Statement	ETV Only (n)	ETC Only (n)	Both Initiatives (n)
1. Opportunity	77 (31)	81 (62)	83 (18)
2. Learn	81 (32)	85 (62)	82 (17)
3. Relations	75 (32)	82 (62)	94 (18)
4. Willing	81 (32)	82 (62)	94 (18)
5. Common	84 (32)	47 (60)	78 (18)
6. Inspired	77 (31)	80 (60)	89 (18)
7. View	81 (32)	81 (62)	94 (18)
8. Credibility	59 (29)	67 (61)	59 (17)
9. Trust	59 (32)	70 (60)	67 (18)
10. Go Along	91 (32)	71 (59)	82 (17)

Stable Constituency. Mayors Rhea and Echols and city managers Lanford and Allen played leading roles in using community-wide strategic planning to create and sustain a coalition of three overlapping clusters of citizens: (1) theme group participants, (2) business and civic leaders, and (3) the general public. The mayors and city managers were aided by the efforts of several city council members as well, including Winston Searles, Osbey Roddey, and Henry Woods. These city officials identified themselves as progressives who supported using city government to promote economic development and quality-of-life initiatives. Quality-of-life initiatives they supported included building more public parks, building walking trails, purchasing public art, providing financial support to cultural events and institutions, promoting historic preservation, beautifying the city through landscaping and forestry, and supporting an affordable housing initiative.

The first cluster supporting the progressive agenda consisted of the large majority of citizens who participated as members of the six theme groups used in ETV and ETC. The data in Table 4.2 on statements three, four, five, and six confirm the positive effects of these planning processes. Statements seven and eight are also useful measures of the support these participants were ready to offer progressive leaders. First, 83.2 percent of these participants "agreed" or "strongly agreed" that they "developed a more positive view of Rock Hill's citizens, especially the business, civic, neighborhood, and political leaders. Second, 63.9 percent of these participants "agreed" or "strongly agreed" that the "openness and credibility of . . . the initiatives helped me to set aside doubts and skepticism about them." The data in Table 4.3 also indicate the majority of participants involved in ETV only, in ETC only, and in both initiatives "agreed" or "strongly agreed" with statements seven and eight.

The second cluster supporting progressive city officials consisted of a variety of business leaders and civic leaders through the years who could mobilize private sector resources to help implement specific initiatives, as well as influence public opinion. The RHEDC has led the effort to promote quality economic development by building high amenity business parks and purchasing downtown properties in order to prepare them for sale to private developers. The large majority of the 50 or more business and civic leaders that have served on the RHEDC's Board of Directors were consistent supporters of ETV/ETC initiatives. The leaders of York Technical College, Rock Hill School District No. 3, Winthrop University, The Rock Hill Chamber of Commerce, and York County were also supportive of the ETV and ETC planning processes. They secured their board or council's unanimous approval in 1990 of a resolution endorsing ETV's plan. And they pledged to implement ETC's plan in 1996. The leaders of the Catawba Indian Nation were the only sponsors to withdraw gradually from participating in ETC's implementation. The most common explanation for the Catawba Nation's diminished commitment to ETC was their focus on matters specific to their community, including improving housing and other basic services in their community and their need to resolve internal conflict over the leadership of the Catawba Nation.

The data in Table 4.4 presents an overall assessment by 13

steering committee members and three members of the city's planning staff of the sponsoring organizations' contributions to ETV and ETC (note that all sponsors had at least one leader among the respondents). The respondents were clearly disappointed with the Catawba Indian Nation's contributions. They did not think the Catawba Nation played an "important" role in doing the ETC process. They also were not "satisfied" with the Catawba's effort during the planning process and with implementing specific initiatives. York County received the lowest ratings of the original seven ETV sponsors, although the satisfaction ratings are above 2.5 which indicate that the respondents were closer to being "satisfied" with the York County's effort than "dissatisfied." The city and

Table 4.4 Steering Committee and Planning Staff Views of Sponsors' Contributions to the ETV/ETC Processes and Implementation

Organization	Topic 1	Topic 2	Topic 3
City of Rock Hill	4.0	3.8	3.8
RHEDC	3.9	3.9	3.9
York Technical College	3.4	3.5	3.5
Winthrop University	3.3	3.4	3.3
Rock Hill School District	3.2	3.0	2.9
Chamber of Commerce	3.2	2.9	3.0
York County	2.4	2.7	2.8
Catawba Indian Nation (ETC Only)	2.3	2.4	2.3

Notes: Thirteen steering committee members and 3 planning staff responded to questions using four-point scales: 1 = very unimportant, 2 = unimportant, 3 = important, and 4 = very important; 1 = very dissatisfied, 2 = dissatisfied, 3 = satisfied, and 4 = very satisfied. The three topics were: Topic 1 = "Importance of doing the ETV/ETC planning process;" Topic 2 = "Satisfaction with support provided for doing the ETV/ETC planning process;" Topic 3 = "Satisfaction with support for implementing specific recommendations in the plan."

the RHEDC were clearly recognized as the most important sponsors of ETV and ETC, and respondents were "very satisfied" with the city and the RHEDC's efforts to develop a plan and implement it.

The general public was the third cluster of citizens who supported the vision defined by ETV's plan. As discussed in Chapter 3, the hundreds of citizens from over 70 community organizations who toured the Belk Building in 1989 in order to see the theme group displays and the models depicting the content of ETV were impressed with the plan.[16] Survey research by Broach, Mijeski, and Associates and by the Palmetto Municipal Benchmarking Project, an endeavor of the Institute of Public Affairs at the University of South Carolina, provide additional evidence of long-term public support for some of the key ideas found in ETV.[17] The key ideas included city beautification, downtown revitalization, business park development, expanding support for the arts and culture, and park maintenance and development. The results of these surveys are discussed thoroughly in Chapter 5. These surveys consistently found general satisfaction with nearly all basic services and a consistent majority favored at least "holding-the-line" on spending. Even during the changing financial conditions in the 1990s, when the city began to reduce its use of electric utility revenue to finance general fund services, only a minority of respondents favored cutting services.

In addition to these three clusters of citizens, the editors of *The Herald* consistently supported progressives by publishing editorials supporting the strategic planning process and many specific initiatives as well. *The Herald* also provided extensive coverage of the ETV and ETC processes and of specific initiatives. This coalition of three overlapping clusters of citizens, the support of *The Herald*, and the momentum gained by establishing a record of success enabled progressive public officials to implement many of the most significant ETV-related initiatives throughout the 1990s. When progressive city officials encountered reluctance or opposition to initiatives, no matter if this challenge came from one or more of the sponsors, or conservative city council members, or conservative citizen activists, or conservative business leaders, they were able to work through this conflict from a position of strength. Although characterized by progressives as a "vocal minority," conservatives have been one or two council seats away from being able to stop the progressives. That conservatives did not take control of council, win the mayoralty since 1985, oppose doing the ETV and ETC planning processes, or even prevent the implementation of some of the main ETV-related initiatives, is testament to the political skill of progressive city officials. City officials skillfully mobilized their coalition of three overlapping clusters of citizens to support progressive candidates and initiatives.

Continuing Citizen Participation

As a "stakeholder" in the community, the public is an integral part of a community-wide strategic planning initiative.[18] This type of planning depends upon extensive citizen participation in order to develop ideas, build a consensus, and secure the resources needed to implement the plan. Mary Walsh believes "bringing people together to determine who they are as a community is the most creative and exciting aspect of community building."[19] In promoting the creation of "deliberative communities," Michael Briand argues that a "community cannot make lasting progress toward solving its problems unless it involves members of the community."[20] Richard Box suggests "one way out of the cycle of intercommunity competition and intracommunity factional conflict is through greater citizen involvement."[21] All of these perspectives reflect an appreciation for citizen participation founded on democratic theory. And so the framework used to assess the participatory structure of a community-wide strategic planning initiative should rest on democratic theory. Jeffrey Berry, Kent Portney, and Ken Thomson offer such a framework.[22]

Berry, Portney, and Thomson integrate the work of Robert Dahl on democratic theory and Benjamin Barber on participation in a democracy to produce a framework that measures the breadth and depth of participation.[23] Breadth means "the extent to which an opportunity is offered to every community member to participate at every stage of the policymaking process."[24] Broad, participatory structures provide citizens "open access to the agenda, extensive information about alternatives, and high rates of participation among the population."[25] By depth they mean "the extent to which the citizens who choose to participate have an opportunity to determine the final policy outcome by means of the participation process."[26] A deep participatory structure is one that offers "equal weight given to all citizen preferences, decisions made on the basis of those preferences, translation of those preferences into final policy outcomes, and effective implementation of those policies."[27] Although developed to measure the "participatory structures" evident in neighborhood-based participation efforts in five cities, their framework is sufficiently broad to allow its application to community-wide strategic planning.

A successful community-wide strategic planning initiative, from the start of the planning process through efforts to update the plan, should achieve a broad and deep participatory structure as described by Berry, Portney, and Thomson. First, the initiative should routinely provide the public with information, be open to any citizen interested in participating, and as John Clayton Thomas suggests, be open especially to "all organized and unorganized groups of citizens or citizen representatives who (a) could provide information . . . useful in resolving the issue, or (b) could affect the ability to implement a decision by accepting or facilitating implementation."[28] However, the public's participation and interest in the initiative need not be constant, especially during the implementation of the plan. A reasonable expectation is that the public's focus will be event-oriented, revealing greater interest, for example, during the implementation of a particular project featured in the plan.[29] Second, achieving broad-based community support for the planning process and the plan itself depends on involving citizens who are representative of the community. As Ronald Thomas, Mary Means, and Margaret Grieve argue, "building a consensus about a community's future means finding ways to engage the interest and commitment of people of all income and educational levels, political persuasions, and occupations."[30] Three types of representation are especially important: (a) geographic (from all neighborhoods in the community), (b) demographic (from different racial, ethnic, and economic identities), and (c) political (from different political parties and interest groups). Third, some projects featured in the plan ought to reflect the ideas of the citizens participating in the planning process and should be implemented as well. Key questions are: Were steering committee members, theme group participants, and the public kept informed during the implementation of the plan?; Did the public at least reveal an event-oriented interest in the initiative?; If the plan was updated, did the public participate?; If so, were the participants in the revision effort representative of the community?; Did citizens who participated think community leaders went along with the most important recommendations in the plan?

Informing and Interest. The city and other sponsors provided information about ETV/ETC through public meetings and occasional newsletters. But these leaders recognized that the numerous articles published in *The Charlotte Observer-York Edition* and especially in *The Herald* provided the public with the greatest amount of information. The steering committee members and city planning staff were satisfied with the quantity, accuracy, and fairness of the coverage by the press. They believed the public had ample opportunity to become well-informed about the ETV and ETC planning processes, the challenges and opportunities facing Rock Hill, the proposals to address these challenges and opportunities, the details in the final plans, and the implementation of projects. They also recognized, however, that most of the public revealed greater interest and knowledge about specific projects as they were being completed, rather than for the planning processes and the whole range of projects in the plans.

Public Participation. The theme group participants were generally representative of the diversity of Rock Hill's community elite, and on some measures, they were representative of the general population. They were leaders of more than 30 different community organizations, including the Sierra Club, the Junior Welfare League, the Fine Arts Association, the League of Women Voters, Rotary, United Way, the Mid-Town Preservation Association (later called Historic Rock Hill), and the NAACP. They were primarily white, males, professionals and business leaders, but women and minorities were significantly involved. Women were 28 percent of the 124 ETV participants and 48 percent of the 176 ETC participants, and minorities were 15 percent of ETV participants and 19 percent of ETC participants (see Table A.1 in the Appendix). Professionals and business leaders dominated both ETV and ETC with government and civic leaders amounting to less than 20 percent of the participants. Citizens working "blue collar" type occupations did not participate on theme groups (see Table A.2 in the Appendix). Theme group members represented a mix of Democrats, Republicans, and Independents (see Table A.3 in the Appendix). The participants also represented all areas within the city, although some wards predominated. In ETV, ward four had the most participants and wards one and three the least (see Chapter 3). In ETC, Wards four and six had the most participants and Wards two and five the least (note that ward boundaries under ETC were different due to redistricting after the 1990 census).

Recommendations. The data reported in Table 4.2 for questions nine and ten indicate theme group participants believed the city's political leaders were "open to my ideas and my interests" and "citizens in positions of power or authority have been willing to go along with many of the most important recommendations in ETV and ETC." Although more respondents disagreed on these two statements than on statements one through seven, the mean responses for both questions are greater than 2.5 and about 62 percent and 78 percent of the respondents "agree" or "strongly agree" with the statements, respectively. The data in Table 4.3 also indicate the majority of participants involved in ETV only, in ETC only, and in both initiatives "agreed" or "strongly agreed" with statements nine and ten.

Achieving Tangible and Intangible Results

If there is a bottom-line to determine success, it is the achievement of results, both tangible and intangible. Bryson argues "creating a strategic plan is not enough. Developing effective programs, projects, action plans, budgets, and implementation processes will bring life to the strategies and create real value for the organization (or community) and its stakeholders."[31] Chrislip and Larson suggest a "successful collaboration produces results, not just structures and activities that create the illusion that a problem is being addressed."[32] As a form of collaboration, community-wide strategic planning can help overcome intangible problems, such as cynicism, mistrust, and parochialism, because it uses a wide range of participation and information sharing practices that have produced such intangible changes in the social capital of other communities.[33] Key questions are: What specific projects and policies from the original plan were implemented?; What specific projects and policies from the revised plan were implemented?; Did the initiative help produce among participants a culture built on trust, reciprocity, civic engagement, and optimism, and one focused on the broader interests of the community?

ETV Projects. The sponsors implemented dozens of major projects promised in the plans. Many projects required the action of only one sponsor. Winthrop University renovated campus facilities throughout the 1990s. The York County Regional Chamber of Commerce located its new headquarters in downtown Rock Hill in 1999. The Rock Hill School District No. 3 implemented the middle school concept in 1991. York County participated in landscaping the I-77 corridor. Yet they also chose not to do so on occasion, such as the school district's decision in 1991 to locate its headquarters outside of the city rather than in downtown as called for by ETV.[34] City officials also had to continue to negotiate with sponsors for their support on initiatives that involved those institutions directly in partnerships with the city. The sponsors' different missions and constituencies presented a coordination challenge to the city's leaders as they sought their cooperation. Below are described some of the more challenging projects either because they were controversial, or because they required the cooperation of several sponsoring organizations, that were implemented.

(1) The city council unanimously adopted a historic preservation ordinance that established the Rock Hill Historic Review Board in 1988. Over the years, the city has created several historic districts and adopted

rules governing the rehabilitation of buildings in these districts.

(2) All seven sponsors of ETV have been involved with "Jubilee: Festival of the Arts," which began in the Fall of 1990. The festival is coordinated by the Rock Hill Arts Council and has become a popular multi-cultural event offering a diverse range of performances, exhibits, and art sales.

(3) The city council unanimously agreed in 1990 to alter its spending guidelines for the accommodation tax revenues. The city decided to provide 25 per cent of this revenue to the Rock Hill Arts Council in order to help this civic organization promote the cultural goals found in ETV.[35] The spending guidelines were again altered in 1998, but the Arts Council continued to receive an allocation of 20 percent from the accommodation tax.

(4) The city council unanimously agreed to establish the Rock Hill Joint Venture On Affordable Housing Corporation in 1990. The city allocated CDBG money to fund the non-profit corporation which offers a first-time home buyers loan program, a home repair loan program, and sponsors volunteer groups who repair homes provided by the corporation.

(5) The city and the RHEDC built Gateway Plaza which is a landscaped entrance to the city along the Dave Lyle Boulevard that features two 60-foot-high, Egyptian revival columns covered in terra cotta tiles and four bronze sculptures produced by New York sculptor Audrey Flack. The two columns were part of the Masonic Temple in downtown Charlotte, which had been razed to make room for the new First Union office building. First Union donated the columns to Rock Hill. Each of Flack's sculptures is of a winged female figure over twelve feet tall named "Civitas." Each "Civitas" holds a symbol of the city: culture, education, textile industry, and function. A fifth "Civitas" sculpture is displayed in the lobby of the renovated city hall. This controversial project was completed in 1991 and cost $1.2 million.

(6) The city renovated city hall by adding a new wing, remodeling offices, removing asbestos, adding a rotunda, and building a new public square. This controversial project was completed in 1992 and cost about $8.5 million.

(7) York County agreed to help finance York Tech's Baxter Hood Continuing Education Center, a 40,000 square foot multi-purpose facility appropriate for conferences, meetings and banquets.

(8) The RHEDC purchased 23 properties in downtown Rock Hill at a total cost of about $2 million. Then it managed the dismantling of the TownCenter Mall's roof beginning in 1993, the installation of new utilities and a streetscape in 1994, and sold all but one of its downtown properties

to private investors by 1999. The RHEDC continues to help recruit private investment to the downtown.

(9) The City of Rock Hill and York County agreed in 1994 to operate the airport through a joint city-county commission and to build a new $1.3 million terminal which opened in 1998. Other renovations to the Rock Hill-York County Airport included a new instrument landing system, new approach lights, and an extension of the runway to 5,500 feet.

(10) The RHEDC's decision to build its fourth business park, the high-amenity, 400 acre Waterford Business Park along the Catawba River and I-77, generated a lot of controversy. The RHEDC completed the initial phase of project in 1995 and other features of the project, including a golf course, a passive recreation area called River Park, and residential home sites, were completed by 1999. A private developer built the golf course and homes.

(11) Winthrop University, York Tech, the RHEDC, and the city worked together to build 9.4 miles of walking and biking trails by 1999.

ETC Projects. ETC incorporated many of the projects unfinished under ETV, such as building River Park, building a new airport terminal, and encouraging the city and the county to adopt similar land-use regulations to better control growth along Rock Hill's boundaries. An important example is the I-77 Corridor Plan adopted in 1998. This plan extends the values and the approach to economic development found in ETV to the area adjacent to Interstate 77. I-77 is the main highway linking Charlotte, NC to Rock Hill. The plan covers the area surrounding I-77 from the Catawba River Bridge on the northern boundary of Rock Hill to Highway 901 just south of the city. The plan also incorporates some of the unfinished projects found in the ETV plan. These projects included spending $11.6 million to install new utilities and a new streetscape along North Cherry Road, which has been Rock Hill's main commercial corridor and its most frequently used access to (and exit from) I-77.[36]

Many community leaders think ETC's biggest success was the neighborhood empowerment program. From 1995 to 1999, Rock Hill increased the number of active neighborhood groups (i.e., neighborhood watch groups, homeowner associations, neighborhood associations) from six to 63.[37] Each group chose its name, defined it boundaries, and set its agenda. With the help of city staff, the most active groups formed the Rock Hill Council of Neighborhoods, which consisted of 18 full-member organizations as of 1999.[38] The basic purpose of the program is to offer better services to neighborhoods by improving the flow of communication between city staff and citizens, and among city staff about how their work affects neighborhoods.

Civic Culture. The ten statements listed in Table 4.2 measure the extent to which the culture in Rock Hill rested on trust, reciprocity, civic engagement, optimism, and the broader interests of the community. The data indicate that the large majority of theme group participants agreed that ETV and ETC promoted these elements in Rock Hill's civic culture. City officials and leaders of the other sponsors believed using community-wide strategic planning helped to create a climate for resolving differences and promoting efforts to cooperate. ETV and ETC did not eliminate conflict, nor was it intended to do so. Rather ETV and ETC were alternatives to conventional approaches used in Rock Hill and other cities to resolve differences, such as negotiating project-specific partnerships not integrated into a community-wide strategy, or using electoral politics to gain control of city, county, and/or school governments. Dennis Merrell, President of York Tech, captured the sentiment about ETV and ETC's impact when he explained the emphasis on balancing interests:

> We needed to promote education, parks and recreation, the arts, and quality economic development and in the process find the appropriate balance. Community-wide strategic planning is the critical tool we used to work with political officials to find this balance. It was never a question that York Tech should get everything it wants; rather we recognized the need to balance what we got with the needs of other community organizations.[39]

Establishing a Governance Network

Community-wide strategic planning rests on an understanding of governance that sees the interdependence of the for-profit, not-for-profit, and government sectors of society. In order to meet the needs of its members, a well-governed community depends upon organizations to form intergovernmental and intersectoral partnerships. Skillful use of community-wide strategic planning can enhance the capacity of communities to act to solve problems,[40] and generally enhance the civic infrastructure present in every community, but that is underdeveloped in many of them.[41] The National Civic League defines the civic infrastructure as the "formal and informal processes and networks through which communities make decisions and attempt to solve problems."[42] The civic infrastructure concept is similar to the concept of a governance network

found in organization theory. Karen Hult and Charles Walcott explain
that:

> ... governance networks link structures both within and
> across organizational boundaries. [They] . . . may be
> permanent or temporary, formal or informal. They may
> be consciously designed, emerge unplanned from the
> decisions of several actors, or simply evolve.[43]

    An important outcome of a successful community-wide strategic
planning initiative should be a governance network (civic infrastructure)
that is consciously planned and permanent (at least for the duration of the
original designated planning period, such as ten years). The members of
this network should establish a partnership that moves beyond information
sharing and isolated efforts to cooperate on one or more projects. Instead,
their partnership should at least reveal an effort to coordinate the
commitment of resources, and perhaps even delegate some of their
individual authority to the network in order to achieve their shared
agenda.[44] Finally, no matter which sponsoring organizations are
responsible for specific actions, Sorkin, Ferris and Hudak argue the key to
a successful implementation is linking the strategic plan to the
organizations' policy making processes, especially budgeting, so
"implementation becomes part of everyday operations."[45] Key questions
are: Did the steering committee meet periodically during the
implementation period?; Did sponsoring organizations integrate parts of
the plan into their routine policy-making processes?; Did the sponsoring
organizations work together to implement specific parts of the plan?; Did
the leaders of sponsoring organizations use formal and informal channels
of communication to maintain the partnership over time?

    The evidence indicates the answer to all of these questions is yes.
The steering committee served its purpose. The sponsors' budgeting,
planning, and other policy-making processes reflected their role in
implementing ETV and ETC. The sponsors formed various partnerships
to implement many ETV and ETC projects. The governance network
lasted the ten years required to see most of ETV's plan implemented. The
resiliency of Rock Hill's governance network and the use of formal and
informal communication channels perhaps is best illustrated in the
discussion of issues arising in the 1990s, such as using tax increment
financing to promote development, that are explored in Chapter 5.

Summary

The implementation of ETV did achieve much of its promise. Rock Hill produced the kind of measurable results recognized in the literature on public sector planning, collaborative decision-making, and governance theory. Competent use of community-wide strategic planning is certainly part of the explanation of Rock Hill's success. But there is more to this story. The competent practice of politics in all of its manifestations is the key to understanding why Rock Hill accomplished so much with this planning tool. To understand how politics and planning were skillfully conjoined in Rock Hill, one needs to explore how the city's public officials practiced leadership in the political process.

Chapter 5

Political Factions and Regime Formation

In order for a governing coalition to be viable, it must have a capacity to mobilize resources commensurate with the requirement of its main policy agenda.
- Clarence N. Stone, Marion E. Orr, and David Imbroscio

Stone, Orr, and Imbroscio argue that regime-building is not a market-like process in which "numerous shortsighted transactions produce a set of governing arrangements."[1] No "invisible hand" exists to move citizens to form coalitions capable of governing their communities. Rather Stone, Orr and Imbrocscio suggest "we have a political process in which leadership may be exercised and purposive choices made regarding how to go about community governance."[2] We see in Rock Hill a community whose public officials, especially its mayors and city managers, provided the kind of leadership needed to establish a redevelopment regime by 1970 and to expand that regime's purpose to include a middle-class progressive agenda in the 1990s.

The Origin and Expansion of the Regime's Purpose

Rock Hill's pluralist regime began as a redevelopment regime under the leadership of Mayor Dave Lyle, who served as mayor from 1964 until 1978. The city council and City Manager Max Holland, who retired in 1979 after serving for fourteen years, deferred to Lyle's leadership. Lyle is reported to have been an outspoken, determined leader who knew the details of policy, supported government initiatives to change Rock Hill, and was in control of the city administration. Even his critics would agree that he went beyond James Svara's director type of facilitative mayor to function as a chief executive.[3]

Svara defines a facilitative mayor as "the guiding force in city government who helps insure that all other officials are performing as well as possible and that all are moving in the right direction."[4] He offers four types of facilitative mayor: caretaker, symbolic head, coordinator and director.[5] Svara defines directors as "leaders in the eyes of their councils, the press, and the public, and they use that recognition as a basis for guidance rather than control."[6] Svara believes directors are the ideal-type facilitative mayor for council-manager cities, but he recognizes the lure for some mayors to act as chief executives, an approach more appropriate for mayor's serving in the mayor-council form of government. Chief executives gain the de facto power to employ the city manager, control the appointment of department heads, shape the budget process, and otherwise become a "driving force" type leader.[7] Lyle exercised this kind of "driving force" leadership in Rock Hill until he lost to J. Emmett Jerome in a run-off election in 1977.

From 1979 to 1986, City Manager Joe Lanford emerged as the key public executive who worked with the majority of the city council to maintain the redevelopment regime. During this eight-year period, Mayor Jerome preferred to maintain a low profile and did not play an important role in the major initiatives recommended by Lanford. He won re-election in 1981 defeating council member Melford Wilson, recognized as the leading progressive voice on city council, by about 221 votes out of a total of 2,997.[8] Jerome is remembered as a two-term mayor who exhibited a friendly personality, enjoyed the ceremonial duties associated with the mayoralty, but who showed little interest in the development of government initiatives, the details of policy, or policy advocacy. His practice of voting against the budget each year is indicative of his passive approach to mayoral leadership. Jerome's supporters said he did so as a matter of principle, but his critics suggest it was a political strategy designed to allow him to say he did not support one or more of the contentious items in the budget. Jerome's approach resembles the symbolic head type of facilitative mayor. Svara suggests such mayors stress ceremonial roles and do not perform the coordinating, communicating, and policy guiding roles needed to be a fully developed facilitative mayor (i.e., a director).[9]

When two-term council member Betty Jo Rhea won the mayoral election in 1985, Lanford found an eager partner willing to expand the regime's agenda. Mayor Rhea ran unopposed in 1989, easily won re-election in 1994, and chose not to run again in 1997. Rhea performed as a coordinator type of facilitative mayor during her twelve years as mayor.[10] Svara defines a coordinator as:

> . . . a team player, keeping the manager and council in touch and interacting with the public and outside agencies, all of which roles contribute to improved communication. Coordinators help achieve high levels of shared information, but since they are weak on policy guidance, they contribute little to policy formulation (at least no more than other members of the council).[11]

Rhea worked as a full-time mayor even though the position is intended to be part-time, which allowed her to excel at the mayor's ceremonial, coordinating, and communication roles. Rhea's mayoral approach complemented Lanford's policy leadership and planning skill.

Rhea and Lanford became an effective executive team and together modified Rock Hill's pluralist regime. From 1987 to 1990, they used ETV to broaden the regime's agenda to include a concern for "middle-class progressivism." This new redevelopment/middle-class progressive regime survived Rhea and Lanford's terms in office. In 1995, Rhea worked with City Manager Russell Allen, hired after Lanford retired in 1993, to use ETC as a means to celebrate ETV's successes, to update the plan, and to start a neighborhood empowerment program. Some Rock Hill leaders characterized ETC as a scaled-down version of ETV and thought it had less of an impact on the community as a result. Yet, the neighborhood empowerment program achieved the most success of any ETC initiative.

After Rhea decided not to run for re-election in 1997, council member Doug Echols won a close mayoral election over council member Kevin Sutton. Mayor Echols had served on city council from 1980 to 1984. He lost a bid for re-election in 1983 in part due to his strong support for building Cherry Park, one of the major quality-of-life initiatives in that era.[12] Echols returned to council in 1994 and in 1997 received Rhea's strong support to be her successor.[13] In his first term, Echols ably performed the ceremonial, coordinating and communicating roles associated with facilitative leadership, and he revealed a keen interest in the policy initiating and organizing roles. Echols clearly wanted to serve as a director type of facilitative mayor.[14] Echols did not devote as much time as Rhea did to the ceremonial roles, although he understood their importance, and tried to balance his part-time mayoral duties with his full-time occupation.[15] Echols' partnership with City Manager Allen, along with his relationship to strong-willed council members, indicates that he did not, and indeed could not, have acted as a chief executive.

Echols collaborated with Allen to promote a variety of issues on the redevelopment/middle-class progressive agenda. Together they developed the I-77 Corridor Plan in 1998 discussed in Chapter 4. Reflecting on the city's successful development of four business parks and the revitalization of downtown, Echols said of the I-77 Corridor Plan that "Our success has not been by accident. Our success has come from a shared community vision and steps taken together."[16] Mayor Echols won re-election in 2001 with 83 percent of the vote. His first order of business was to help the council replace Allen who announced his resignation in Fall 2001 in order to become city manager of Raleigh, NC.

Defining Issues in Rock Hill Politics

The development of Rock Hill's pluralist regime has been shaped by several economic, social, fiscal and political developments since the 1970s. First, as mentioned in Chapter 1, the main economic challenges confronting the city were:

(1) the decline of downtown as a retail center beginning in the 1970s;

(2) the closing of 11 out of 13 textile plants by the early 1980s which helped create an unemployment rate of 13 percent in 1982;[17] and

(3) controlling the investment in undeveloped areas in and along the border of the city in the 1980s and 1990s, especially along the roads linking Rock Hill to a new interstate highway (I-77), in order to prevent urban sprawl.

Second, social challenges arose partly from the influx of new residents in the 1980s many of whom brought new perspectives about community and politics. Third, the flow of intergovernmental aid and the city's revenue from the sale of electricity presented financial advantages in 1980s, but in the 1990s, relying on revenue from the sale of electricity became problematic. Fourth, in the late 1970s and again in the late 1980s, African American residents demanded greater representation in city government. As a result of this political challenge from the minority leaders, Rock Hill changed its electoral system twice in order to better incorporate African American citizens into city government. The first change was from a partisan, at-large system of electing council members prior to the 1979 elections to a partisan system using three wards and three at-large seats from 1979 to 1989. The second change was to a non-partisan/all ward system from 1989 to the present.

These challenges, especially those stemming from economic and social change, created a sense of "crisis" that stimulated an expansion of the regime's purpose. By the mid-1980s, Rock Hill was no longer a stable, prosperous textile community of long term residents, and city leaders struggled to help the community adjust to this new reality.

Factions in Rock Hill's Politics

Politics in Rock Hill, at least as far back as the 1960s, is best characterized as competitive issue-oriented politics between two factions within the Democratic Party: progressives and conservatives.[18] The Democratic Party had so dominated city elections that the Republican Party did not field candidates for city council or mayor until the mid-1990s, and even then Republicans could do so only informally because the city had adopted non-partisan elections in 1989. To be successful in Rock Hill politics prior to 1989 meant winning a competitive race within the Democratic primary. Although most elections have been competitive, voter turnout normally has been low, which is typical of municipal elections across the nation. Because some precincts include voters who live outside the city's boundaries, it is not possible to report precise participation rates for city voters. Estimates indicate turnout of registered voters to have been 30 percent in the 1970s and early 1980s, 40 percent in the 1985 election, and less than 20 percent in the late 1990s.[19]

In the course of campaigning, candidates have used appeals that readily identified themselves as either progressives or conservatives. Once on the council, the large majority of progressives and conservatives debated issues without undermining personal relationships, and more often than not, were able to work well together. Although most matters before council through the years have been resolved routinely and by unanimous votes, some of the important issues were decided by four-to-three or five-to-two votes, including:

(1) approving the budget each year;
(2) hiring Assistant City Manager Russell Allen to be city manager in 1993;[20]
(3) allocating $65,000 to match a state grant in 1994 to buy the property needed for construction of River Park;[21]
(4) rejecting a motion to re-allocate money from "street-scaping" projects in three downtown historic districts to pay for a new fire station in 1996;[22] and
(5) using a tax increment district to finance the North Cherry Road Development Project in 1998.[23]

The Progressives

Since the 1970s, progressives consistently advocated using city government as the agent to attract investment to Rock Hill and especially to the downtown. Some of the progressive's initiatives included:

(1) participating in the national government's Model Cities Program from 1969 to 1973;
(2) covering Main Street with a roof in order to create TownCenter Mall in 1977;
(3) constructing the Dave Lyle Boulevard to serve as the "gateway" to downtown;
(4) joining nine other municipalities in 1979 to form the Piedmont Municipal Power Agency (PMPA) in order to buy an interest in the Catawba Nuclear Power Station;
(5) creating the RHEDC in 1983 in order to build business parks the city needed to attract business investment; and
(6) building Cherry Park (a 68 acre park containing a 1.5 mile walking and biking trail, five multi-purpose recreational fields, five professional softball/baseball fields, a playground, and picnic areas) which opened in 1985.

Beginning in Fall 1987, the progressives used community-wide strategic planning (i.e., ETV) to expand the pluralist regime's agenda beyond economic development to include quality-of-life initiatives. These initiatives included building more public parks, building walking trails, purchasing public art, providing financial support to cultural events and institutions, promoting historic preservation, beautifying the city through landscaping and forestry, and supporting an affordable housing initiative. By pursuing this agenda, progressives hoped to create a new identity for Rock Hill in order to avoid becoming a stereotypical suburb. They understood that the scope of this agenda had to rest on a broad-base of interest group and public support. ETV helped produce the coalition capable of carrying-out many of the items on the progressive's agenda. Mayors Rhea and Echols and City Managers Lanford and Allen provided the executive leadership for the progressive faction in the 1980s and 1990s. They were joined by several council members: Melford Wilson (1978-1984), Doug Echols (1980-1984; 1994-1998; mayor 1998-present), Winston Searles (1980-present), Henry Woods (1982-1994), and Osbey Roddey (1990-Present). These progressive city officials used ETV to create a coalition consisting of three overlapping clusters of citizens: business and civic leaders; theme group participants, and the general public. These three clusters of citizens, combined with the support of the editors of *The Herald*, gave Rock Hill's progressive leaders an advantage in any conflict with conservative leaders.

Cluster One: Business and Civic Leaders   Progressive city officials were supported by a variety of business leaders and civic leaders through the years who could mobilize private sector resources to help implement specific initiatives, as well as influence public opinion. Table 5.1 displays a list of some of these lawyers, bankers, developers, business executives, and civic leaders who were identified during interviews as important to ETV's success and/or who were quoted in news articles supporting ETV-related projects. Many of them have served on the RHEDC's Board of Directors, whose size has varied over time, but has had at least thirty members. Many of them also have served on the RHEDC's eight member executive committee, which essentially "runs" the organization, and consists of the city manager, two city council members and five board members. The leaders of the five institutions that joined the city and the RHEDC in sponsoring ETV in 1988 also have played important roles during ETV's implementation and updating through ETC.

Of all the leaders of these other five sponsors, Dennis Merrell, President of York Technical College since 1989, stands-out as the most consistent advocate for ETV. He has been one of the key champions advocating the use of community-wide strategic planning in Rock Hill to produce a high quality-of-life for citizens. He also defended many of the cultural, historic, and economic initiatives that generated controversy, arguing they contributed to a balanced approach to development in Rock Hill. The leaders of the other sponsors - Rock Hill School District No. 3,

Table 5.1 Business and Civic Leaders Supporting Progressive Initiatives

Name	Organization	RHEDC
Marty Cope	J. M. Cope Construction	Yes
Bobby Belk	Belk Construction Company	Yes
David Rogers	D. L. Rogers Construction/	
	Main Street Properties	No
H. P. Skip Tuttle	Coldwell Banker —	
	The Tuttle Company	Yes
Bill Neely	Capital Corporation	Yes
David Vipperman,	Rock Hill Business Technology	
	Center	Yes
H, Butch Honeycutt	First Union Bank	Yes
Lud Vaughn	Bank of America (Nations Bank)	Yes
C. John Hipp	Rock Hill National Bank	Yes
Dennis Stuber	First Citizens Bank	Yes
Cecelia Gardner	First Union National Bank	Yes
W. Mark DeMarcus	Wachovia Bank	Yes
Robert Thompson	Springs Industries	Yes
Marshall Doswell	Springs Industries	No
Clarence Hornsby	Bowater Corporation	Yes
Barre Mitchell	Bowater Corporation	Yes
James Simpson	Thistledown Gallery	Yes
Jim Hardin	Kennedy, Covington, Lobdell and	
	Hickman Law Firm	Yes
Don Harper	Harper, Peterson, Rogers & Reno	
	Law Firm	Yes
Vicki Huggins Cook	Executive Director, Rock Hill Arts	
	Council	Yes
Manning Kimmel	WRHI/WRHM Radio	Yes
Harry Dalton	Star Paper Tube Company/Sierra Club	No
Barbara James	Historic Rock Hill	No
Grazier Rhea	Historic Rock Hill/Catawba Regional	
	Planning	No
Wayne Patrick	Publisher, *The Herald*	Yes
Terry Plumb	Editor, *The Herald*	No
Carl "Buzz" Elliot	Executive Director, Rock Hill	
	Chamber of Commerce	Yes
Sylvia Ayers	Board Member, Rock Hill Arts	
	Council	No
Nate Barber	Winthrop University/Small Business	
	Development	Yes

Winthrop University, The Rock Hill Chamber of Commerce, and York County - were also supportive of the ETV planning process and secured their boards' (or councils') unanimous approval in 1990 of resolutions endorsing the plan. As discussed in Chapter 4, these sponsors did implement many of ETV-related initiatives, including many joint projects. But their support for specific ETV-related initiatives varied during the 1990s, which presented the city's progressive officials with a coordination challenge. The greatest challenge facing the city involved securing the cooperation of the county and the school district to help finance economic development projects.

The use of a tax increment district to finance economic development projects affected the short-run revenues (e.g., a 15 year period) received by the school district and the county. A tax increment district allows a city to borrow money through a bond sale to pay for improvements in the district and then use the increased property tax revenue derived from new investment in the "blighted" area to pay off the debt. Tax increment financing was not controversial when Rock Hill used it to finance the building of TechPark in 1988, a business park located in a area encompassing an abandoned textile mill property, and to finance the redevelopment of downtown.[24] These two blighted areas produced little new tax revenue because of the lack of new investment. The county and school district were willing to forego the small amount of new tax revenue possibly generated by the area in its current condition in order to gain more revenue in the future once the area attracted investment after the city made improvements. Basically they decided to allow their share of any new tax revenues from those two areas to be used to pay for the improvements in those areas.

When the city proposed in 1991 to use a tax increment district to finance the building of Waterford Business Park, a business park and golf course development on 400 acres along the Catawba River and I-77, York County and Rock Hill School District No. 3 officials objected. County and school officials did not want to give up their share of property tax revenue generated by the new Galleria Mall, which the designated area included. Although the state enabling law allowed for areas that are not blighted to be included in the district, such as the Galleria Mall, county and school district officials were reluctant to give-up their tax revenues for 15 years.[25] They were not confident the Waterford project would be successful. They also had anticipated in their budget planning receiving the revenue from the successful Galleria Mall.

The city decided to negotiate with school officials. Mayor Rhea explained "We would like it to be a win-win situation rather than being at odds. This is important to the future for the people of Rock Hill and the state of South Carolina."[26] City officials achieved an agreement that gave the school district and the county each their share of tax revenue through January 1994 and their full share of personal property taxes for the entire 15 years of the district's life. School superintendent Joe Gentry said of the compromise, "I didn't say I was happy. It is the best possible solution I can think of though. To be totally happy, I wish it wouldn't have an effect on our tax base."[27] Phil Kelly, the school's associate superintendent of administration, said of the deal, "Basically, we are gambling that they [the city] are going to have development in that area; otherwise we get nothing down the road."[28]

All phases of the Waterford project have been completed. The high amenity business park opened in 1995. The 200-acre Waterford Golf Course built by a private firm on land donated by the RHEDC opened in 1997. A private developer built residential home sites between the business park and the golf course and River Park, a 70 acre passive recreational area, opened in 1998. The tension generated over the use of tax increment financing resurfaced again when the city proposed the North Cherry Road Development Project in 1998.

This project was an important part of the I-77 Corridor Plan and involved installing underground utilities, high quality street lighting and traffic signals, storm-water management improvements, and landscaping. City officials presented the North Cherry Road Development Project to county and school officials before introducing it to the public. The county and school district officials praised the project but objected to tax increment financing for reasons similar to the ones they had raised in the Waterford dispute. Initially the city council approved the tax increment district in a five-to-two vote in December 1998.[29] As they had done in the Waterford project dispute, city officials continued to negotiate to secure the cooperation of the county and the school district to share the cost of improvements along North Cherry Road.

In January 1999, the negotiations broke down and York County filed a lawsuit over tax increment financing (the school district did not formally join the suit but informally supported it). County Council Chairman Carl Gullick expressed regret about filing the suit, but felt the county had to exercise its "fiduciary responsibility."[30] City, county, and school officials promised to keep talking. After seven months, the city and county settled the lawsuit out of court.[31] Both the city and county councils unanimously approved the settlement, which calls for the city to pay $10.8 million and York County to pay $5.3 million to fund the project, and a tax increment district will not be used. Rather the city will use proceeds from the sale of land, CDBG money, among other sources, and the county will use accommodation tax revenues and other sources as well. All three governments will continue to receive property tax revenues from the area. City, county and school district officials all regretted the lawsuit. They considered it the "low point" in their relationships. Yet they all embraced the settlement because the project promises to change North Cherry Road in ways envisioned in ETV and ETC. Rather than serve as the end of the partnership that began in ETV and continued through ETC, the settlement rekindled the idea of working together.

Cluster Two: Theme Group Participants The second cluster supporting the progressive's agenda consisted of the large majority of citizens who participated as members of the six theme groups used in ETV and ETC. These citizens were generally representative of the diversity of Rock Hill's community elite, and on some measures, of the general population. The readiness of 274 theme group participants to support the progressive agenda is evident in data from my 1999 survey. I discussed the results of this survey in Chapter 4 and presented the data in Table 4.2. The large majority of the 113 ETV/ETC theme group participants who responded to the survey confirmed the positive effects of these community-wide strategic planning processes. The mean for each of the statements is above the 2.5 mid-point on the four-point scale, and the percentage of participants agreeing or strongly agreeing with each statement ranges from 62.3 to 84.1. Two statements are especially useful measures of the support these participants were ready to offer progressive leaders. First, 84.1 percent of these participants agreed or strongly agreed with the statement: "I became more willing to contribute my time, effort and other resources to help Rock Hill become a better place to live and to work." Second, 80.9 percent of these participants agreed or strongly agreed with the statement: "I was inspired by ETV and ETC to do my part to make the plans a reality."

Cluster Three: The General Public The general public is the third cluster of citizens who supported the vision defined by ETV's plan. As mentioned in Chapter 3, the citizens who toured the Belk Building to view the plan in 1989 overwhelmingly supported the plan. Surveys conducted in the 1980s and 1990s also provide important evidence of long-term support for ETV proposals.

Broach, Mijeski, and Associates contracted with the city to conduct a telephone survey of 343 people in 1987 with a margin of error plus or minus five percent.[32] Respondents indicated the importance of six projects using the following scale: not important, somewhat important, and very important. The majority of respondents thought it was "very important" to improve traffic flow (81 percent), re-pave and maintain streets (88 percent), beautify the city (62 percent), assist the downtown area (56 percent), attract industry (85 per cent), and expand water, sewer, and electric services (63 percent). The 1987 data reported in Table 5.2 indicate that a large majority of people also were "satisfied" or "very satisfied" with basic services, but that some services could be improved. The appearance of roads and street maintenance had the lowest ratings, which indicated a public readiness to pursue improvements in those service areas.

As part of the ETV planning process in July 1988, Broach, Mijeski, and Associates contracted with the city to conduct a mail survey of the 700 businesses belonging to the Chamber of Commerce in order to measure their opinion about the "business climate" in Rock Hill.[33] The mail survey had a 28 percent response rate. The business community's responses mirrored the general public's opinion on several issues. Seventy-six percent of the respondents thought having a "strong economic base in downtown" had a moderate to high level of importance, and 63 percent of the respondents rated Rock Hill's downtown as "poor." Ninety-seven percent of the respondents thought the "visual appearance of the city" had a moderate to high importance, and 44 percent and 15 percent rated Rock Hill's appearance as "fair" and "poor", respectively. Eighty-nine percent of the respondents thought "arts/cultural offerings" had a moderate to high importance, and 39 percent and 8 percent thought Rock Hill's cultural offerings were "fair" or "poor", respectively. Clearly business leaders thought these three indicators of the business climate were important and needed to be improved. Four other indicators received high ratings of importance: "local government supportive of business (82 percent)," "economic development programs (60 percent)," "local government services (55 percent)," and "local government taxes (61 percent)." And the large majority of business leaders awarded Rock Hill excellent or good ratings on each of these four indicators: (69 percent, 77 percent, 63 percent and 68 percent, respectively). Broach, Mijeski, and Associates found these ratings were consistent across all types of businesses.

The results of the 1987 and 1988 surveys indicate the general public and the business community were ready to support many of the initiatives that eventually became part of ETV. Progressive city officials were in the position to use ETV to craft a coalition capable of supporting

Table 5.2 Assessment of City Services (Percentages Reported)

Service	1987	1994(n)	1998(n)	1998(n)
Water	90	92(320)	...	...
Planning	83	...	...	...
Appearance of Entry Roads	50	...	...	...
Amount of City Services	88	...	...	...
Park Maintenance	94	...	...	...
Cherry Park	...	98 (281)	...	...
Other City Parks and Fields	...	89 (204)	...	...
Greenways and Trails	...	90 (167)	...	...
Garbage Collection	84	83 (312)	72(212)	8(212)
Street Maintenance	60	65 (315)	...	...
Fire Protection	96	99 (299)	93(196)	1 (196)
Police Service	78	94 (310)	53(209)	16(209)
Storm Drainage	76	79 (300)	...	...
Electric Service	...	80 (322)	...	...
Sewer Service	...	92 (318)	...	...
Neighborhood Centers	...	83 (162)	...	...
General Satisfaction	...	93 (340)	...	...
City Services Overall	...	...	61(212)	8(212)

Notes: Broach, Mijeski, & Associates used four responses in 1987 and 1994: very dissatisfied, dissatisfied, satisfied, and very satisfied. The percentages reported here are for a combined total of satisfied and very satisfied responses. They do not report the "n" for 1987 data. The Palmetto Municipal Benchmarking Project used a five-point scale in 1998: excellent, good, fair, poor, very poor. The first 1998 column reports the combined total of excellent/good responses and the second 1998 column reports the combined total of poor/very poor responses.

an agenda that went beyond delivering basic services, because citizens were largely satisfied with the city's performance. The time also was ripe for expanding the agenda beyond economic development to include a range of quality-of-life initiatives.

Broach, Mijeski, and Associates did three surveys during the implementation of ETV. In 1992 they contracted with the Chamber of Commerce to measure public opinion regarding downtown.[34] Broach, Mijeski and Associates did a telephone survey of 309 people with a margin of error of plus or minus five percent. They found that 70 percent of the respondents favored removing the roof of TownCenter Mall, and only 18 percent opposed this idea. They also reported that 50 percent of the respondents "never" shop downtown. Instead, 56 percent of the respondents shop at the Galleria Mall located along the Dave Lyle Boulevard adjacent to the exit off of I-77, and 23 percent shop at stores along the North Cherry Road corridor. The survey results confirmed the death of downtown as a retail center, and provided support for the idea of converting the downtown into a location for office space, restaurants, cultural facilities, apartments, and selective retail shopping.

Broach, Mijeski, and Associates' 1994 survey was similar to the 1987 survey and again asked respondents to assess services and offer budget priorities.[35] They did a telephone survey of 342 people on behalf of the city. As was the case with the other telephone surveys, the margin of error for the 1994 survey was plus or minus five percent. The 1994 data reported in Table 5.2 suggest a marked improvement in police services compared to 1987, and high levels of satisfaction with nearly all basic services. It is important to note that in this time period conservatives were complaining about the management of the electric utility system (see below), yet 80 percent of the public were "satisfied" or "very satisfied" with their electric service. Finally, the 1998 data from the survey by the Palmetto Municipal Benchmarking Project reported in Table 5.2 confirms the large majority of Rock Hill citizens were "satisfied" or "very satisfied" with the basic services they received from the city.[36]

In their 1987, 1994 and 1997 surveys, Broach, Mijeski, and Associates also asked respondents to offer their spending priorities on various services.[37] Data reported in Table 5.3 indicate that respondents wanted more spent on services in 1987 than they did in 1994, with the exception of wanting even more spending on police in 1994. By 1997, the large majority of the respondents wanted to keep spending the same, rather than increase or decrease spending. Yet there existed a sizable minority view in 1997 that ranged from 11 to 48 percent that favored spending less on several services, including landscaping, forestry, parks and open

Table 5.3 Spending Preferences on City Services (Percentages Reported)

Project	More 1987	More 1994	More 1997	Same 1987	Same 1994	Same 1997	Less 1987	Less 1994	Less 1997
Streets and Sidewalks	76	60	...	24	37	...	1	3	...
Economic Development	...	64	...	...	28	...	...	8	...
City Beautification	...	20	...	...	48	...	...	32	...
Landscaping/Horticulture	...	...	11	...	...	73	...	...	14
Forestry	...	...	16	...	...	65	...	...	19
Parks and Open Spaces	24	27	21	65	59	68	11	14	11
Recreation	31	...	...	62	...	...	7	...	...
Swimming Pools	...	...	6	...	...	68	...	...	26
Sports	...	...	11	...	...	69	...	...	20
Arts and Crafts	...	...	5	...	...	47	...	...	48

(continued)

Table 5.3 Continued

Project	More			Same			Less		
	1987	1994	1997	1987	1994	1997	1987	1994	1997
Community Centers	...	...	13	...	...	68	...	...	19
Garbage, Trash, Recycling	33	26	...	64	67	...	3	7	...
Curbside Waste	...	...	5	...	...	70	...	...	21
Recycling	...	...	14	...	...	64	...	...	19
Fire	42	22	17	57	75	74	1	3	7
Police	61	65	26	37	33	66	2	2	6

Notes: Broach, Mijeski, & Associates used three responses to measure spending priorities in 1987 and 1994: less, same, more. In 1997, they used three similar responses: reduce, continue, increase. For ease of comparison I use the 1987/1994 terms to report 1997 data. They did not report the "n" for questions in 1987 or 1997. They did report the "n" for 1994: Streets and Sidewalks = 296; Economic Development/Jobs = 285; City Beautification/landscaping = 299; Parks and Open Spaces = 260; Garbage, Trash, and Recycling = 304; Fire = 282; and Police = 300.

spaces, recreation services, community centers, curbside waste collection, and recycling. The changing financial conditions of the city in the 1990s, which are discussed in Chapter 6, helps explain this shift in 1997 towards a "hold-the-line" on spending viewpoint. Yet it is important to remember that only a minority of respondents favored cutting services.

The Conservatives

The conservative faction was reluctant to use city resources in what they perceived to be risky ventures incapable of re-directing market forces. The conservative faction preferred to emphasize basic services, keeping utility rates low, ending the transfer of electric utility revenues to support basic services, avoiding tax increases, avoiding new debt, and allowing the private sector to re-build Rock Hill's economy. Some conservatives were not as concerned about the city's image and did not take seriously the progressive's rhetoric about a "new" Rock Hill. Mayor Jerome and council members Maxine Gill (1978-1982; 1994-Present), Bidwell Ivey (1984-1994), Hugh Harrelson (1982-1998), Bill Thomas (1984-1994) and Kevin Sutton (1994-Present) have been the main city officials leading the conservative faction in the 1980s and 1990s. Of this group, Thomas took the least visible role, rarely expressing strong opposition or asking tough questions about ETV-related initiatives, and he often voted with the progressives even when Ivey and/or Harrelson did not. Since 1994, Gill and Sutton have not only voiced strong support for conservative ideas, but they offered motions to cut services or alter budget allocations to reflect an emphasis on basic services, and routinely voted against the budget in order to demonstrate their opposition to some of the items in it.[38]

Conservative city officials have been supported by a group of business leaders led by developers Warren Norman and Ralph Norman. The Normans have taken a high-profile role through the years. They have regularly criticized a wide range of city initiatives, including the use of tax increment financing, annexation efforts, new sign ordinances, building business parks, the RHEDC's management, and the management of the city's electric utility. Other business leaders have joined them on certain issues, especially the city's management of the electric utility, such as motel owner John Pharr, restaurant owner Vince Houston, and Piedmont Medical Center executive director, Paul Walker (see Chapter 6). Some business leaders have voiced strong support for conservative candidates during elections, such as restaurant owner Larry Bigham, his wife Kathy

Bigham, and developer Greg Whitehead's support for Kevin Sutton in the 1997 mayoral contest.[39]

The conservative perspective also has been supported by citizen-activists critical of the progressive's agenda, such as Steve Rast and Jane Davenport. They have appeared at council meetings, written letters to the newspapers, and run for office. Rast led a petition drive in 1992 to demand a referendum on a $6.4 million bond issue designed to finance removing the TownCenter Mall roof, among other projects (see Chapter 6). Although the petition drive did not secure enough valid signatures to force the city to have a referendum, it did secure 1,492 valid signatures which indicated a large minority of citizens were willing to support a conservative critique of the city's financial management practices. In 1994, Jane Davenport ran for city council against incumbent Searles for the Ward 1 seat. Searles easily won that election, but Davenport received 197 votes and won three of the nine precincts in the ward.[40]

Election results for mayor from 1973 to 2001 also provide some measure of the public's support for conservative leaders. In five of the eight mayoral elections, 1973, 1977, 1981, 1985 and 1997, conservatives were competitive in a majority of the precincts. Conservatives won the mayoralty in 1977 and 1981 and nearly won in 1973, 1985 and 1997. The 1973 election won by progressive incumbent Mayor Lyle, the 1977 election won by conservative Jerome and the 1997 election won by progressive Echols were settled in run-off elections. Mayor Jerome won re-election in 1981 by 221 votes out of a total of 2997 votes cast and progressive Betty Jo Rhea won her first term in 1985 by only 324 votes out of a total of 4272 votes.[41]

In the 1997 election, council member Sutton decided to run for mayor at the age of 27. During his mayoral campaign, Sutton criticized numerous progressive initiatives especially the city's spending on ETV-related initiatives. He criticized spending $8.5 million to renovate City Hall, buying the sculptures at Gateway Plaza, building the Waterford Business Park, landscaping historic districts, funding cultural events, subsidizing arts organizations, and using electric utility revenues to pay for basic services. He showed little interest in celebrating the achievements and updating ETV. For example, he chose not to participate in ETC in 1995 and commented in a brief interview in 1999 that he did "not know anything about it."[42] In his mayoral campaign, Sutton stressed spending money on basic services, such as fire and police services and neighborhood parks, and avoiding tax increases. Sutton won the plurality of votes in the first round of the election, but he lost the run-off election by less than 200 votes to Doug Echols.

In the 1989, 1994 and 2001 mayoral elections conservatives were not competitive. Mayor Rhea did not have opposition in 1989 and in 1994 she defeated conservative activist Steve Rast by about 1000 votes. Rast did receive 1,469 votes which is some measure of the conservative faction's base in the electorate during the height of her popularity.[43] In the 2001 election, two African American candidates, Tom Colter and Baxter Tisdale, challenged Mayor Echols, but they received minimal support. Echols easily won re-election with 83 percent of the vote. During the campaign Echols touted his support for the North Cherry Road Development Project and the Saluda Street landscaping and design improvements, as well as his support for continued revitalization of the downtown area. And he repeated the progressive's call first heard during ETV to control growth, because he did not want Rock Hill "to be a community that continues to sprawl and come to look like Anywhere, USA."[44]

Summary

Clearly, the electoral success of conservative candidates for city council and their competitive efforts in mayoral elections over the years suggests a vibrant opposition existed to the progressive's pluralist regime. One need only recall Jerome's narrow victories in the 1977 and 1981 mayoral elections and the narrow losses of conservative candidates in the 1973, 1985, and 1997 mayoral contests. This opposition even existed when the pluralist regime's agenda focused on redevelopment and promoting economic growth, as it did in the 1970s and for most of the 1980s. Although characterized by progressives as a "vocal minority," conservatives have been one or two council seats away from being able to stop the progressive's effort to broaden the pluralist regime's agenda to include middle-class progressive ideas. That conservatives did not take control of council, win the mayoralty since 1985, oppose doing the ETV planning process, or even oppose implementing some ETV-related initiatives, is testament to the political skill of progressive city officials. Progressives successfully mobilized their coalition of three overlapping clusters of citizens to support progressive candidates and initiatives, and worked effectively with the media.

Chapter 6

Conflict, Cooperation and Issue-Based Politics

Skill in politics is the ability to gain more influence than others, using the same resources.
- Robert A. Dahl

The progressive's success in securing conservative council members' support, or at least acquiescence, on some initiatives, and the conservative's occasional success in challenging progressive ideas, is illustrated by discussing prominent issues in Rock Hill politics. Progressive and conservative leaders generally agreed on an approach to electoral reform to satisfy African American demands for political incorporation, and on doing the ETV planning process. As far as the details of the plan, conservatives were skeptical and often critical of certain ETV initiatives. They were especially critical of the city's role in the RHEDC and of the city's management of the electric utility fund. Electoral success of ardent conservative candidates in the mid-1990s indicates the on-going vulnerability of the progressive's agenda to the electoral process.

The Politics of Race in Rock Hill

The differences between progressive and conservative factions within the Democratic Party have not been defined by the politics of race. Since the 1970s both factions have campaigned for African American votes. And their appeals to African American voters were generally the same as for all voters. Each faction stressed how their approach to government would benefit African Americans, as well as the rest of Rock Hill's citizens. And each faction had some success in winning African American votes. For example, in the late 1980s and early 1990s, some African American leaders wanted to see better services targeted to their neighborhoods. These desired services included spending more on storm water management, road repair, sidewalk construction, housing rehabilitation, and park improvements, before money was spent on city beautification, public art, business parks, and other ETV initiatives.[1] The conservative faction's agenda was quite compatible with these service priorities. Other African American leaders defended the breadth of the progressive agenda as well as promising to deliver better services to minority neighborhoods.[2]

Each faction's approach to addressing Rock Hill's economic and quality-of-life concerns, however, was not the African American leaders' highest priority. Representation on city council was the paramount issue for African American leaders in the late 1970s, late 1980s and the early 1990s. Although their substantive policy concerns were being addressed in the political process, African Americans wanted to achieve a more complete level of political incorporation. Rufus Browning, Dale Marshall and David Tabb define three levels of political incorporation: no representation at all, some representation on a council dominated by a coalition opposed to the racial minority's interests, and "the strongest form of incorporation - an equal or leading role in the dominant coalition that is strongly committed to minority interests."[3] African American leaders in Rock Hill worked to achieve the highest level of political incorporation. This meant having representatives on council and having those officials play an important role in the faction that governed the city.

Although African Americans were one-third of Rock Hill's population, no African Americans served on council under the at-large electoral system used prior to 1979. During the debates about changing the electoral system, white leaders of both factions expressed the traditional arguments supporting the use of at-large elections. They argued that council candidates would be more likely to speak to the broad interests of the community in at-large elections, rather than to the narrower concerns of particular areas within the city. Yet, both conservatives and progressives eventually supported a compromise in 1978, and again in 1988 when the issue re-surfaced.

In a referendum in 1978, voters overwhelmingly approved the use of the mixed system (i.e., three ward seats, three at-large seats, and the mayor directly elected at-large). Under this plan in 1979, two African Americans were elected to council. Frank Berry won an at-large seat and Winston Searles won a ward seat. In 1981 Berry did not win re-election. Searles won re-election throughout the 1980s and 1990s. Over the years, Searles has voted consistently with the progressive faction and used his influence to direct improvements to his ward as well. One important example is the renovation completed in 1995 of the auditorium in the Emmett Scott Neighborhood Center, formerly a high school that the city purchased in 1972 and converted to a neighborhood center.

African American leaders were not satisfied with the mixed system. City officials from both factions, including Mayor Rhea of the progressive faction and council member Harrelson of the conservative faction, expressed strong support for using the mixed system. But under pressure from African American leaders and the United States Department of Justice, white leaders of both factions again compromised and endorsed changing to an all ward system (with the mayor elected at large). Indeed, in 1988 city council voted unanimously to support this change. Mayor Rhea explained that "It is the best long-term solution. It is a way we can move ahead quickly and get this settled."[4] And Harrelson suggested "We are in a position to control our own destiny. And I believe the people of Rock Hill are going to unify behind the council and support the plan. The people of Rock Hill want to look to the future."[5]

Although turnout was only four percent of registered voters, voters approved overwhelmingly the all ward system in April 1989.[6] In the Fall 1989, African American candidate Osbey Roddey won election to council, and like Searles, continues to serve. Roddey has consistently supported the progressive agenda in the 1990s, and like Searles, has become an important progressive leader. Both have served as the city's representatives on the eight member executive committee of the RHEDC. They also have directed projects to their wards, such as the Crawford Road improvement initiative in the early 1990s, which is part of both of their wards, and the Saluda Street improvement initiative, which runs through their wards as well as through part of Ward 3, and involves landscaping, removing abandoned cars, demolishing deteriorated housing, new street lighting, new sidewalks, and placing utilities underground.[7] Yet hopes for a third African American on city council have not been realized in the 1990s.

The 1991 and 1993 elections were delayed by the United States Department of Justice until April 1994 due to the NAACP's effort to have the wards drawn in such a way as to help elect a third African American to the council. As part of the settlement between the city and the NAACP, Ward 3 became the third ward to have an African American majority. In spite of having a majority, African American candidates supported by progressives have lost each election to conservative Kevin Sutton, in part because voter turnout was low, and because Sutton did a good job of getting his supporters to the polls. Clearly, the future of the redevelopment/middle-class progressive regime depends upon the continued support of the African American electorate.

Support for ETV

In addition to finding common ground with progressives when addressing African American complaints about the electoral system, conservative council members also were willing to support using community-wide strategic planning as a tool to address the city's future. For example, in 1988 Ivey defended the amount of money being spent on ETV's planning process (over $200,000) suggesting that "The money is well spent from the standpoint we're getting a lot of Rock Hill citizens involved. There is interest and enthusiasm. I don't know that the city can afford to do all the recommendations, but it gives us a goal, something to shoot for."[8] After seeing the presentation of the plan at a retreat in 1989, Harrelson suggested "I think we all need to go back home and digest it. I think we need to take it to the people and do a selling job and get their reaction."[9] This pattern of general support for ETV lasted well into the 1990s, and perhaps reflected the conservatives' realization that the progressive's agenda was popular with community leaders and the public. This pattern of support also reflected the dire economic conditions facing the city in the 1980s.

The conservatives' general support for ETV co-existed with their skepticism and their desire to proceed cautiously. They reserved judgment about specific projects in order to assess whether the city could afford them. And they continued to raise questions about the city's financial management practices throughout the 1990s. Building Gateway Plaza, subsidizing the Rock Hill Arts Council and approving the $6.4 million bond needed to finance the downtown's revitalization in 1992-1993 are good examples of Thomas, Ivey, and Harrelson's willingness to support some ETV-related initiatives, but only after expressing caution and asking tough questions.

Gateway Plaza and Public Art

Gateway Plaza is the landscaped entrance to the city along the Dave Lyle Boulevard completed in 1991 (see the description in Chapter 4). Of the three conservative council members, Ivey is the only one to have offered unqualified public support in 1990 for the four sculptures calling them "magnificent."[10] Harrelson expressed some concern that the sculptures seemed out of place and could not be enjoyed because of their being along a busy highway. He also worried about vandalism, but expressed strong support for the rest of the plaza's design.[11] Gateway Plaza's price tag eventually rose to about $1.2 million. Of this total, only the sculptor's fee (kept confidential, but rumored to be less than $40,000) was covered through private donations from firms located in TechPark, one of the city's business parks adjacent to the Gateway.[12] The city used revenue from the tax increment district used to build TechPark to pay most of the costs of the plaza's construction. In 1996, Gateway Plaza received one of 36 awards issued jointly by the National Endowment for the Arts (NEA) and the U.S. Department of Transportation for designs that link public art and transportation planning.

Subsidizing the Rock Hill Arts Council

ETV included an emphasis on promoting the cultural life of the community. Some of the cultural initiatives received the unanimous support of the council, such as starting Jubilee: Festival of the Arts and using accommodation tax revenue to finance arts programming. Conservatives also supported the creation of a Center for the Arts. In 1991, the city council unanimously supported the allocation of $300,000 to match the $150,000 grant from the NEA to support the Arts Council's effort to establish a Center for the Arts. The RHEDC donated the building along Main Street in downtown that after a $720,000 renovation became the Center for the Arts.[13] The Center opened in 1996 and is a state-of-the-art facility, home to the offices of the Rock Hill Arts Council, classrooms, eleven artist studios to be rented out, and gallery space.

Before the Center was completed, however, the Arts Council leased the city-owned "old federal building" and paid the city a rent of

$100 per month, which was well below the cost of utilities for the building, about $27,000 in 1993.[14] The Arts Council started leasing the space in 1987. When the lease came up for renewal in 1993, Ivey expressed opposition to subsidizing the Arts Council, which had a budget in 1993 of $94,000. Ivey demanded to see how much the subsidy cost the city and wanted the public to know as well. Although he initially voiced strong opposition, Ivey still voted to renew the lease in 1993 without any changes in the subsidy.

Financing Downtown Revitalization

The $6.4 million bond issue to finance the revitalization of downtown Rock Hill, as well as several other projects, is another important and controversial ETV-related initiative supported by the three conservatives on council.[15] One-third of this money was to pay for removing the TownCenter Mall roof and re-opening Main Street. In the 1970s, Mayor Lyle and city staff pushed for the creation of TownCenter Mall as a way to revitalize retail shopping in the downtown. By the late 1980s, the TownCenter Mall had lost most of its 33 stores. City Manager Lanford, who as assistant city manager had advocated building the mall, now supported its demolition. Lanford explained that it "was the right option in 1977 because it extended the life of the retail business in downtown by ten years."[16] He also suggested one of TownCenter Mall's unintended positive effects was "to save several historic buildings (and their facades) that might otherwise have been remodeled or demolished had a different revitalization plan been adopted in the 1970s."[17] Conservative Maxine Gill, the most out-spoken critic of city initiatives, argued it was a failed policy and waste of taxpayer's money, and she continues to be proud that as a citizen-activist she opposed the project in 1977.[18] Although removing the roof using public money appeared popular in 1992, even with conservatives, some citizens rallied against the bond issue claiming that the city could not afford the additional debt.

Steve Rast led a petition drive to force a referendum on the bond issue. Rast claimed to support some of the projects to be funded, but insisted that citizens should be permitted to vote on the bond issue. Downtown business owner Jim Bazemore co-chaired the Committee for a Better Rock Hill, which organized an effort to oppose the Rast petition drive. Bazemore and his supporters circulated fliers defending the city's finances, extolling the various projects to be funded through the bond issue, and asking citizens not to sign the Rast petition. In the end, Rast's group obtained 1,492 valid signatures, just 315 short of what they needed.[19] In this "heated" political climate, Ivey, Harrelson, and Thomas all voted in favor of rejecting the petitions and going forward with the bond issue. This decision to support the public financing of the project represented a shift from their wait-and-see attitude evident during the ETV planning process and in the first year of ETV's implementation.

For example, in 1990 all three voted against spending $7,500 to hire an architect to prepare plans to renovate the city-owned "old federal building" (i.e., the former post office) in downtown Rock Hill.[20] They wanted to have a better sense of how the downtown would be re-developed before the city started spending a lot of money renovating city-owned buildings. Mayor Rhea and other progressives on the council wanted to have the city lead in the re-investment in downtown. Rhea argued "We've reached a point where we have to make some bold decisions. We did this when we had to go ahead and vote on Cherry Park."[21]

By 1992 the conservatives' skepticism about spending public money to lead the revitalization effort had been replaced by a guarded optimism that their progressive colleagues on the council were right to go forward with the revitalization of downtown. Several factors may have influenced this shift in opinion. In 1991, the Chamber of Commerce, with the help of the RHEDC, established a downtown business and property owners' task force that worked towards a consensus on the future of downtown.[22] Results of a survey in 1992 by Broach, Mijeski, and Associates suggested the public and the business community were ready to move forward. Finally, the successful counter attack on Rast's petition drive by the Committee for a Better Rock Hill indicated significant support of downtown business interests, as well as the public's support, for moving forward with the downtown revitalization project.

Two Major Controversies

Although persuaded to support the Gateway Plaza project, the Arts Council, and investing in downtown, Ivey, Harrelson and Thomas continued to express their skepticism and cautiousness through persistent questioning and occasional opposition to other specific ETV-related initiatives. Conservatives also raised questions about the city's role in the RHEDC and the city's financial practices.

The RHEDC Controversy City Manager Lanford, with the support of a majority of council members, worked with the business leaders from the Chamber of Commerce in 1982 and 1983 to create the non-profit RHEDC. Although not an outspoken opponent of this initiative, Mayor Jerome did not play an important role in the RHEDC's creation, or during its first few years of its operation. Over the years, the city government has provided funding to the RHEDC by allocating CDBG money, selling bonds to finance projects, and staffing the corporation with city employees. The RHEDC also has used profits from its sale of land in its business parks to finance new projects in the city. The RHEDC has built four business parks. The 100-acre Airport Industrial Park opened in 1984. The 200-acre Southway Industrial Park opened in 1988. The 250-acre TechPark opened in 1988. And the controversial 400-acre Waterford Business Park opened in 1995 (note that acreage totals do not include roadways and common areas). Between 1988 and 1990, the RHEDC also purchased 23 properties in downtown Rock Hill at a total cost of about two million dollars. Then it managed the dismantling of the TownCenter Mall roof beginning in 1993, the installation of a new utilities and a streetscape in 1994, sold all but one of its downtown properties to private investors by 1999, and continues to help recruit private investment to the downtown area. In spite of the appearance of success, the RHEDC was a target of sharp criticism throughout this era.

In the late 1980s and early 1990s, some conservatives questioned the city's plan to revitalize the downtown by working through the RHEDC. They were reluctant to let the RHEDC use city funds to buy-up downtown properties, as a first step towards building a new downtown. For example, in 1989 developer Eddie Aberman expressed skepticism about using public money to initiate rebuilding downtown in part because of the already low value of rental property. He did not think private investment would follow. Aberman suggested: "I've never been a great proponent of spending a lot of money [in the downtown] even though we have property down here and would benefit."[23] Some conservative council members, especially Harrelson, echoed this desire to see if the private sector would invest in the downtown before taxpayer dollars were spent.[24]

Conservatives also questioned the city's role in staffing and financing the RHEDC, as well as the range of projects it pursued. For example, in 1992 council member Harrelson criticized the RHEDC for initiating the Waterford Business Park project (see description in Chapter 5) during a recession without having any tenants committed, and at the risk of overbuilding office space in the region. Harrelson explained that the "economic development corporation works out these projects, then comes to [city council] for the money. And that's why I say the RHEDC takes the council's vote for granted. They think we're going to rubber-stamp it.

And I have no intention of rubber-stamping."[25] Ivey also complained about the RHEDC saying that "I just don't have enough information about the development corporation. You don't want to stand in the way of progress, but you do want to have a handle on how the money is being spent . . . ."[26]

Both these council members were expressing the same misgivings presented by developers Warren Norman and Ralph Norman. The Normans were suspicious of the RHEDC financial transactions, such as the RHEDC donating land to a private company to build the golf course in the Waterford project, and they opposed the RHEDC's efforts to build business parks in general. Ralph Norman criticized the Waterford project stating "We are concerned that the city is getting into areas that they're taking a loss on and the only way they're going to pay for it is to increase utility rates and increase property taxes. We get hit either way."[27] Mayor Rhea countered these charges explaining that the city has no intention of using utility revenues to pay for non-utility improvements in this project. Revenue from the tax increment district would be used to finance non-utility improvements at Waterford.[28]

Stephen Turner served as the RHEDC's executive director from 1988 to 1996, and was a key advocate for ETV and the implementation of ETV-related initiatives. Turner explained "the ultimate purpose of the Rock Hill Economic Development Corporation is to stimulate and direct economic growth. This means attracting new jobs and not just any jobs, but higher paying jobs."[29] The Waterford project was in step with the RHEDC's economic development strategy. And he defended public investment in downtown revitalization arguing "a nice downtown will also help attract people to the business parks. Downtown needs to create the impression that this community cares about itself."[30] Turner also worked with the RHEDC's business leaders and with progressive city officials to defend the RHEDC from its critics.

For example, when conservatives were vigorously questioning the city's financial practices in 1995, Turner expressed frustration with complaints about the city's support for the RHEDC. He challenged the objectivity of a KPMG Peat Marwick's report to city council recommending the city could save money by billing the RHEDC $62,500 per year to pay for staff salaries. Turner suggested the KPMG consultants spoke to local residents who were RHEDC's most vocal critics, and decided to recommend the salary rebate before talking to him.[31]

Clay Andrews succeeded Turner in 1996 as RHEDC executive director and also routinely defended the non-profit corporation's work. Andrews identified the four ways the city has benefited by being a partner and a primary sponsor of the RHEDC.[32] First, the RHEDC built all of its business parks within the city, and in the long run these areas will produce property tax revenue for the city. Second, the businesses in these parks are customers of the city's utilities. Third, the RHEDC pursues a quality type of economic development that fits within the vision articulated in ETV. Fourth, the RHEDC channels any profits back into projects benefiting the city. If the RHEDC were a private, for-profit company it could choose to build business parks outside the city, just as the Rock Hill Chamber of Commerce did in 1963. If the RHEDC were private, it could decide to purchase electricity from another supplier, just as the Norman development group has done for some of its projects. Private developers also may choose to pursue developments that do not further ETV-related goals for quality development. And finally, private developers retain the profits on their investments rather than re-investing the proceeds into projects that benefit the city.

Progressive public officials and business leaders suggest that the real reason the Normans opposed the RHEDC, and particular projects like Waterford, were their perceptions that the city used public money to compete with them over economic development in Rock Hill. Progressives argued that the city through the RHEDC had to lead in downtown revitalization and in business park development for two reasons: (1) the private sector was not investing in these two areas and (2) the city needed to promote high-quality economic development. The progressives won these debates in the 1990s, and were able to pursue their economic development strategy using the RHEDC, for four reasons:

(1) the lure of "good" jobs to the city's troubled economy appealed to the public;
(2) the success of the three business parks already built by the RHEDC in attracting new firms;
(3) the fact that the Rock Hill School District No. 3 and York County had a "stake" in the success of downtown revitalization and in the Waterford project, because they were being financed via tax increment districts; and
(4) the potential for private property adjacent to downtown and to the Waterford area to increase in value as commercial sites.

The Enterprise Fund Controversy In the early 1990s, conservatives rallied around the effort to end the progressive faction's practice of using enterprise (i.e., utilities) fund revenue to pay for general city services. Conservatives argued this transfer policy made electricity too expensive in Rock Hill and in the long-run might make it difficult for the city to buy its share of electricity required in the PMPA agreement unless rates were increased substantially.[33] City Manager Lanford defended the transfer policy. He argued that the "transfers from the utilities fund to the general fund [is] a dividend to the owners of the utility system who are the citizens of Rock Hill, and the city pays that dividend in terms of lower taxes and increased services to the people. This is a fairer way than having everything paid by property taxes, because everybody does not own property. This spreads the costs over the people who are actually getting the service."[34] From 1983 to 1989, the council followed Lanford's approach and was able to avoid any tax increases to finance city operations. By 1989, 59 percent of the revenue needed to pay for general fund related services came from the enterprise fund. In 1990, the city raised taxes and began to reduce the transfer of enterprise funds. By 1994 electricity revenue paid only 38 percent of the costs for general services. Lobbying by business leaders in 1994 added momentum to reduce the transfer.

The Normans organized a number of business leaders to complain about electricity rates in 1994, including motel owner John Pharr, restaurant owner Vince Houston, and Piedmont Medical Center executive director, Paul Walker. They demanded a thirty percent rate reduction.[35] The Normans and their fellow business leaders also hired an accountant t o study the city's financial management practices and the management of the electric utility system and asked the city to follow the recommendations in his report.[36] One of the accountant's main recommendations called for ending the transfer practice. Mayor Rhea responded suggesting "If you look at the list of things they have recommended, those are the things we have done . . . and will try to do."[37] City Manager Allen commented that "Their concerns are our concerns. We are not at odds. I think we can make them [the business leaders] much more comfortable about how we're addressing those concerns."[38] Although these business leaders did not get their thirty percent reduction, they did create a climate in which electric rates would not be raised and the transfer would continue to be reduced.

In 1995, Standard & Poor's downgraded the PMPA's bond rating from an "A" to an "A-," in part because PMPA cities were transferring too much of their revenue from the sale of electricity to support general city services.[39] Analysts were concerned that the PMPA will be less competitive as a provider of electricity if its member cities needed to keep rates high in order to support their general services.[40] Also in 1995, the city council approved a contract with KPMG Peat Marwick to do a performance audit of the city's operations. The report concluded that the city was well-managed and provided a high-level of services, but could improve in several areas, including reducing its reliance on revenue from the sale of electricity to finance general city services.[41] As a result of these two reports, the city adopted a policy calling for an annual reduction of at least 2.0 percent in the transfer.

In 1996, a group of 25 business leaders led by Jim Hardin, a lawyer, and Manning Kimmel, owner of two radio stations serving Rock Hill, organized the Citizens for Rock Hill's Future.[42] Hardin and Kimmel have been supportive of the progressive's agenda and have been active as RHEDC board members. The group's purpose was to help the city find ways to ease the transition to a reduced reliance on utility revenues, prepare for the coming competition that electric deregulation will bring, and find ways to operate the city more efficiently. City Manager Allen welcomed their help suggesting that he "has been a big supporter of them all along. We want business leaders to understand the city and to help develop our strategy."[43]

By 1999, the city reduced the transfer of electric utility revenue to 17 percent of the general fund expenditures.[44] The reduction of this transfer put financial pressure on the general fund services. Cutting services and/or raising property taxes, various fees, or utility rates were not popular options with council or the public, and so Rock Hill cut costs primarily by reducing the number of employees. The city began "doing more with less" in 1991 by reducing the number of full-time, non-public safety employees each year. By 1999 the city had eliminated 90 of these positions. The total number of full-time employees fell from 721 in 1991 to 633 in 1999. The city also increased revenue by increasing:

(1) the property tax rates one mill in 1991 and four mills in 1998;
(2) the business license fee by five percent in 1999;
(3) the water rates five percent in 1993 and 1998;
(4) the sewer rates about five percent in 1997 and 1999; and
(5) the sanitation fees several times to pay for tipping charges at the county landfill.

Electric rates were not increased at all. The city simply absorbed four to five percent increases in the price of electricity from the PMPA rather than passing the increased costs onto consumers. Although expenditures did increase on general services from about $23 million in 1991 to about $30 million in 1999, expenditures from the enterprise fund increased a greater amount: from about $60 million in 1991 to about $90 million in 1999.[45]

The conservatives' successful attack on the use of electric revenues to pay for general services helped to create a fiscal crisis mind-set among many community leaders. Although conservatives were not able to stop many of ETV-related initiatives in the 1990s, they created the political climate in the late 1990s that was far different from the one in the 1980s and the early 1990s that supported the progressive's agenda. In the 1980s, progressive city officials were able to motivate community elites and the general public to support the redevelopment/middle-class progressive agenda using three basic appeals. First, they appealed to widespread concern about the city's pervasive economic decline. Second, they appealed to the challenge of being a suburban *ring city* of Charlotte threatened with a loss of identity. Third, they appealed to the hope that they could steer market forces to produce quality development. By the mid-1990s, these appeals began to lose their persuasive power. Conservatives raised the prospect of a "fiscal crisis".

Certainly Rock Hill's version of a fiscal crisis was not as substantial as the kind of crisis that changed New York City's regime in the 1970s.[46] Nevertheless, Rock Hill's fiscal crisis created a mind-set in the mid-1990s that could have inhibited the city's ability to maintain the breadth of the progressive's agenda into the first decade of the 21st Century. Some community leaders and public opinion started to shift towards an agenda that stressed resting on the city's success over the past 15 years, and a wait-and-see approach to determine how electric deregulation affected the PMPA's ability to compete in a free market for electricity. Such a shift in the agenda was a perspective more supportive of a caretaker regime. Clearly, the perception of a fiscal crisis had significantly affected electoral politics in the 1990s, just as the economic crisis in the 1980s had created an opportunity for progressive action.

Council Elections: 1987 to 2001

Incumbents Searles, Ivey and Thomas ran unopposed in the 1987 Democratic primary, and there were no Republican candidates, so by winning the primary they were elected. The 1989 council election, which was the first using the non-partisan, all ward system, also did not produce a significant contest between progressive and conservative candidates. Incumbent progressive Henry Woods easily defeated Gary Dye 340 to 230 and incumbent conservative Harrelson ran unopposed.[47] Newcomers Osbey Roddey and Paul Knox, both African American, contended for the remaining seat, which Roddey easily won 325 to 164.

Because the 1991 and 1993 elections were delayed by the U.S. Department of Justice pending the re-drawing of ward boundaries, the city used a special electoral calendar for the next two elections. All six seats on city council and the mayor were up for election in April 1994. Then Wards 1, 2, and 3 were scheduled for October 1995 and Wards 4, 5, and 6 and the mayor were scheduled for October 1997.[48] The 1994 election offered voters several competitive races for council. Echols easily defeated Jewell Eggleston for the Ward 6 seat with 75 percent of the vote. Incumbents Harrelson and Roddey ran unopposed for Wards 4 and 5, respectively. Searles defeated two opponents, one being conservative activist Jane Davenport, for Ward 1 with 67 percent of the vote. The most vigorously contested races involved Wards 2 and 3 in which conservative incumbents Ivey and Thomas were challenged by other conservatives.

Although Ivey had been a conservative voice on council since 1984, and had almost defeated Betty Jo Rhea in the race for mayor in 1985, he lost to fellow conservative Maxine Gill in 1994 by 21 votes for the Ward 2 seat. He lost in part because of his willingness to support specific ETV-related projects. Gill campaigned as the more consistent critic and advocate for conservative views. She called Gateway Plaza, especially the sculptures, a "waste of taxpayer's money," and thought the city should not incur more debt as it had done to finance the rehabilitation of downtown Rock Hill.[49] She thought the city made a "dumb deal" when it approved the $300,000 match to obtain only a $150,000 grant from the NEA to help finance the building of the Center for the Arts.[50] Gill had been a long-time critic of Lanford and the progressive faction in the Democratic Party. As a member of the Democratic Party, she considered herself the "watchdog" the public needed to expose mismanagement, frivolous spending, and possible corruption.[51] Gill's critics described her attacks on Mayor Rhea and City Manager Lanford as unfounded, mean-spirited, and not in keeping with the council norm not to personalize differences about policy, but they represented the views of a vocal minority in city politics. Gill ran unopposed in 1995.

In 1994, Kevin Sutton campaigned using the conservative faction's ideas. He defeated Gwendolyn Finley, an African American woman, by twenty votes in a runoff election for the Ward 3 seat. Incumbent Bill Thomas, a fellow conservative, finished a distant third in the first round of the election. As was the case with Ivey, Thomas' loss can be attributed in part to his support for ETV-related initiatives. Although the city used non-partisan elections, Sutton is widely recognized as the first Republican, and the youngest person, to win election to council.

Finley challenged Sutton again in 1995. She campaigned as a progressive and a consensus-builder who could work well with other council members and with city staff to bring industry to Rock Hill, keep utility rates low, and work to reduce crime.[52] Finley also suggested that as an African American she would better represent the Ward and she expected the support of neighborhood associations and ministers. Sutton defeated Finley by 70 votes. During the campaign, Sutton stressed his record of providing constituent services and his on-going effort to keep electric utility rates low, improve basic services to the Ward, and challenge the administration on fiscal issues.[53]

In the 1995 council election, incumbent progressive Searles faced three African American challengers for the Ward 1 seat. All three challengers ran as fiscal conservatives who would cut spending, better control electric utility rates, and improve infrastructure in the Ward.[54] Searles won re-election by defending his involvement with ETV, especially the downtown projects, highlighting the improvements he brought to the Ward, and staying positive.[55]

In the 1997 council election, progressive incumbent Roddey ran unopposed in Ward 5. Incumbent conservative council member Harrelson did not seek re-election to Ward 4. Newcomers Jim Reno and Rob Herron were elected to council, easily defeating Bill Neal and Tom Roper, respectively. Reno won the Ward 6 seat formerly held by Echols, who became mayor, and Herron replaced Harrelson in Ward 4.

Like Sutton, Reno and Herron represent a new generation of Rock Hill leaders with little knowledge of the problems Rock Hill faced in the 1970s and early 1980s, and of ETV and ETC in particular. Reno and Herron have not been clearly aligned with either the progressive or conservative factions. In their campaigns, both expressed concerns about the city's finances. They opposed raising property taxes, but were open to raising the accommodation tax and small, across the board cuts in programs. They also favored efforts to consolidate city and county services to reduce the duplication of effort. This approach was compatible with the conservative's agenda, which included a critique of the city's finances, an effort to limit new initiatives that may lead to tax increases and a focus on providing basic services (i.e., police).

There also were signs that they were willing to work with progressives. For example, Reno, Herron, and Mayor Echols represented the city in the successful negotiations with York County officials in 1999 to settle the lawsuit over the city's plan to use a tax increment district to finance the North Cherry Road Development Project.[56] This support for the North Cherry Road proposal, which was a key part of the I-77 Corridor Plan, indicated they were open to ideas linked to the ETV/ETC vision. Herron and Reno also were invited to the RHEDC's annual retreat in November 1999, which featured a review of ETV's achievements over the ten years of its implementation, but only Herron attended. Clearly, progressive leaders hoped to persuade Herron and Reno to support some, if not all, of the items on their agenda.

The 1999 election offered voters competitive races in all three Wards, but turnout was still only 15 percent of eligible voters.[57] Early in the campaign, incumbent Searles decided he would not seek re-election in 1999. However, he decided to enter the race at the last minute, claiming constituents were not happy with the other four candidates running.[58] Searles' opponents criticized him for not bringing enough spending back to the district to improve streets and parks, for his role as an RHEDC Board member, for not doing enough to help young people avoid crime, and for being too passive as a council member. As he had done in 1995, Searles defended his record and challenged his opponents to provide the facts to support their claims about his record. Searles led the five candidates with 258 votes, but had to face Jimmy Warner in a run-off election, which Searles won.

Gill and Sutton also had opponents in 1999. Gill easily defeated Tom Fagan and Marty Thomas by earning 70 percent of the vote. Sutton also defeated African American minister, Herb Crump, by earning 60 percent of the vote. As promised in all of their campaigns, Gill and Sutton were much less willing to cooperate with other council members. They were proud to be conservative critics of the progressives' efforts. And they have not demonstrated a high level of confidence or trust in the city staff. They were especially critical of City Manager Allen in the late 1990s, and worked to limit his compensation.

The 2001 election was a status quo affair. Incumbent council members Roddey, Reno, and Herron ran unopposed. All three spoke of the need to promote more cooperation among council members and for the continued re-vitalization of downtown.

Replacing the City Manager

Although the 1999 and 2001 elections did not produce any changes in city council or the mayoralty, replacing Russell Allen was a major test of the progressive's ability to shape the regime's character. The development of effective mayor-city manager partnerships helped the progressive faction a chieve s uccess i n t he 1 980s a nd 1 990s. After an extensive national search, city council chose Carey Smith, City Manager of Daytona Beach, Florida to be the new manager beginning April 2, 2002. Smith's predecessors, Lanford and Allen, were skilled users of community-wide strategic planning. How Smith views planning as a tool to shape the community's future will go a long way towards determining whether progressives will be able to use this tool to nurture the coalition needed to win elections and implement an agenda containing middle-class progressive ideas.

Summary

From the mid-1980s through 2001, progressive leaders won elections and resolved conflicts over policies and programs to their advantage. The one exception to this record of success was the phasing-out of the electric utility revenue transfer to the general fund. Progressives achieved so much because ETV/ETC created the coalition needed to sustain the effort. Conservative council members Ivey and Thomas lost to challengers from their own faction, Gill and Sutton, respectively. Searles withstood serious challenges from conservative candidates and Roddey never faced opposition for his council seat. Newcomers Reno and Herron became the swing votes between the factions, but appeared to be open to development initiatives reflecting the vision defined in ETV/ETC. Community leaders continued to recognize the central role elections played in determining the purposes of Rock Hill's pluralist regime. They all knew that the faction controlling the city council determined the course not only of city government, but also the pattern of public-private relationships affecting Rock Hill's social and economic well-being.

As of 2001, progressives retained majority control of city council and the mayor's office, but the conservative faction continues to be well-positioned to offer a serious challenge. As it has in the past, electoral politics will determine whether Rock Hill's pluralist regime pursues a redevelopment/middle-class progressive agenda, returns to being a redevelopment regime only, or transforms into a caretaker regime controlled by the conservative faction in city politics.

Chapter 7

Using Community-Wide Strategic Planning in the Future

The way a city responds to its external environment is determined, to a considerable degree, by the nature of its internal politics. Different cities make different choices.
- Dennis R. Judd and Todd Swanstrom

The economic, social and political changes affecting Rock Hill since the 1970s were not unique to this city. Many cities of all population sizes across the South, indeed all regions of the United States, confronted some combination of the external challenges facing Rock Hill: the loss of manufacturing firms, sprawling new development, the decline of their downtown as a retail center, population growth pressures, challenges to their cultural identity and intergovernmental rivalries; and some combination of internal challenges as well: such as racial politics, ideological politics, and personal rivalries. Rock Hill was exceptional because of the city's successful effort to use community-wide strategic planning, the most difficult type of planning, as a tool to address these challenges. Rock Hill's progressive leaders skillfully used this tool to create the political coalition needed to develop and to implement a ten-year plan that would transform Rock Hill. Rock Hill's effort achieved five significant results planning and community building theories predict should occur if the tool is used skillfully, including managing uncertainty by promoting learning, resolving conflict, involving citizens, producing tangible and intangible results, and establishing a governance network for the duration of the planning period. Rock Hill achieved these results, because of the competent practice of community-wide strategic planning, visionary leadership, and the commitment of public leadership to the process and to the plan.

Competent Practice

Rock Hill's leaders used standard strategic planning practices skillfully. Using theme groups as a forum for public participation worked well in both planning processes, but especially in ETV. They enlisted key stakeholders to serve on the steering committees for ETV and ETC, and on the theme groups, which helped to assure the commitment of public and private resources to particular projects. They worked skillfully with the news media, especially *The Herald*, to inform the public and to promote the planning processes and the plans. Rock Hill's leaders relied on experts to inform rather than to decide, which prevented a consultant-dominated process and helped build public support for various initiatives. Linking the projects and the programs featured in ETV/ETC to the organizations that needed to implement them contributed to the achievement of many specific projects. Finally, Rock Hill's leaders, especially the public officials, managed conflict over the implementation of projects constructively. Although each city must adapt any model to their own particular circumstances, Rock Hill's success makes ETV/ETC an excellent starting point for cities considering a community-wide approach.

Leadership and Regime-Change

Rock Hill's public officials joined with other key community leaders to exercise what Barbara Crosby has defined as "visionary leadership," which helps a community "interpret current reality, foster a group mission, and shape collective visions of the future."[1] Crosby suggests visionary leaders understand how to "design and use formal and informal forums, places where interpretations of present conditions and future realities can be debated and shared meanings and missions developed."[2] Rock Hill's progressive public officials exercised "visionary leadership" by recognizing the potential of community-wide strategic planning to be used as a tool to alter the way citizens and organized interests interacted to determine how public and private resources would be invested to shape Rock Hill's future. ETV and ETC enveloped to some extent conventional choice processes, such as municipal elections, public hearings, and investment planning by for-profit and not-for-profit organizations. In other words, ETV/ETC created the context in which other choice processes occurred.

Rock Hill's progressive public officials also exercised visionary leadership by using community-wide strategic planning as a tool to build a coalition capable of supporting the implementation of a redevelopment/ middle-class progressive agenda in their pluralist regime. As Stone, Orr, and Imbroscio suggest, the "carrying capacity" of the coalitions supporting caretaker and redevelopment regimes is less difficult to maintain, because of the limited nature of their agendas.[3] The expansive agenda of a middle-class progressive regime; or as in Rock Hill's case, the expansive agenda of a hybrid redevelopment/middle-class progressive regime formed in the late 1980s and sustained through the 1990s, requires a broad coalition to carry out its agenda. Rock Hill's progressive public officials realized in 1987 that winning elections could sustain a caretaker regime, or a redevelopment regime, as was the case in Rock Hill in the 1970s and early 1980s, but not a regime with a middle-class progressive agenda. Rather than rely on elections and other conventional choice processes, they initiated ETV in order to produce the broad coalition and to provide the momentum needed to implement a wide range of progressive initiatives in the community. Rock Hill's progressive public officials have answered in the affirmative Ferman's question: "Can the electoral arena be modified so that it becomes a suitable vehicle for planning?

Public Commitment

Rock Hill's successful use of community-wide strategic planning demonstrates the primary role the public sector has in using this tool in pluralist regimes. Mayor Rhea and Mayor Echols, and City Manager Lanford and City Manager Allen, consistently championed the use of community-wide strategic planning. The majority of the city council consistently supported their efforts. The city provided most of the financial and human resources needed to support the planning processes. The mayors, city managers, and some key council members cultivated public opinion and worked skillfully with other key community leaders to implement the plans produced by ETV and ETC.

If an ETV-like process is used by other cities governed by pluralist regimes, then the city officials leading the dominant coalition will need to monitor changing contextual conditions during the implementation of the strategic plan in order to take the steps needed to maintain the coalition. Changing contextual conditions are likely and arise from several sources. Foremost among these are:

(1) the results from successfully implemented initiatives, such as the new investment in downtown Rock Hill, the public art program, and building new parks and trails; and

(2) social, economic and political developments independent of those initiatives, such as the economic recession in 1991, the conservative's critique of the RHEDC, the changes in the leadership of sponsoring organizations, the perceived fiscal crisis in Rock Hill arising from the conservative critique of the management of the city's electric utility in 1994, and the move towards electric deregulation in South Carolina in the late 1990s.

Public leadership, especially by council members, the mayor, and the city manager, is the key to sustaining the pluralist regime through the years as the context changes. City officials leading the dominant coalition will need to find ways to work through conflict constructively in order to continue to secure the cooperation of coalition partners. And they have to make the key strategic choices: when to delay or eliminate an initiative, when and how to publicize successful initiatives, when to propose new initiatives, who to recruit to run for council and mayor, and who to hire to be city manager. If the agenda of the pluralist regime includes middle-class progressive ideas, as it did in Rock Hill, or even lower-class opportunity ideas, as it may in other cities, then public leadership will be even more important. Rock Hill's progressive city officials practiced this kind of visionary leadership.

Reflecting on ETV's origin, Lanford suggested 1989 "was the point when Rock Hill decided it could be something besides a little, sleepy textile town. We weren't just coming up with a plan for that time. It was a new way to think of our community."[4] Rock Hill's progressive leaders were able to maintain the broad-based coalition needed to achieve much of their vision in the 1990s, and that vision continues to shape policy.

Final Observations

Deindustrialization, sprawling investment in the periphery of metropolitan areas, and the political incorporation of African Americans were trends that challenged many cities across the South in the last thirty years of the twentieth century. This history and analysis of Rock Hill's use of community-wide strategic planning reveals how one city addressed multiple challenges stemming from these trends creatively. Although some parts of ETV/ETC will need to be altered, other cities can certainly learn from Rock Hill's experience. Strategic Planning, especially the community-wide approach, may not be a panacea, but ETV/ETC has demonstrated its value as a collaborative problem-solving tool. ETV/ETC is certainly a "best practice" worth studying.

Rock Hill's case also demonstrates the nexus between politics and community-wide strategic planning. Rock Hill has shown how a pluralist regime, founded in the electoral arena, can expand the regime's agenda to include middle-class progressive ideas by using planning. Ferman's research on Pittsburgh indicates that a corporatist regime founded in the civic arena can use planning involving neighborhoods over several decades to transform a city.[5] Taken together, Ferman's study of Pittsburgh and the Rock Hill case suggest that planning practices involving the community have the greatest chance for success in cities governed by regimes in which public sector leadership is strong, such as in pluralist and corporatist regimes, and in regimes founded in electoral and civic arenas. Will community-wide strategic planning, a special type of planning practice, work well in cities governed by elitist, corporatist or hyperpluralist regimes? Will this planning practice work in regimes founded primarily in the civic, business or intergovernmental arenas? Future research on community-wide strategic planning should address these questions.

Appendix

Research Design

Stage One: 1987-1990

As a resident of Rock Hill from 1987 to 1990 I observed the events associated with ETV. I began collecting information systematically in 1988. Data were gathered using news articles, municipal documents, questionnaires, and structured interviews. Twenty-four important leaders were interviewed in 1990, including 12 of 14 members of the steering committee, the project coordinator, the 6 city council members, both assistant city managers, and three civic leaders. They discussed ETV's history and evaluated the process. In the summer of 1990, questionnaires were sent to all 19 ETV staff members and the 124 citizens who were invited to work on the theme groups in order to obtain their biographical data and their evaluations of ETV. Of 143 questionnaires, 62 were returned for a response rate of 41 percent. All 86 participants in this stage of the study were promised confidentiality.

I obtained basic information needed to describe ETV and document its history from news articles and municipal documents. I read over two hundred news articles and editorials pertaining to ETV printed in Rock Hill's two daily newspapers, *The Herald* and *The York Observer* (part of *The Charlotte Observer*). The numerous municipal documents reviewed included the theme group member's handbook, the five newsletters published during the planning process, the minutes of theme group meetings, and numerous other memos, press releases, and speeches. The evaluation of the ETV planning process discussed in Chapter 3 is based primarily on data from interviews, questionnaires, the Comment - Log placed at the Belk building during the public review period, and 24 letters and idea forms sent by citizens to the city.

Stage Two: 1999-2001

Robert Golembiewski defines three variations of empirical theory common to public administration research.[1] One of those variations, "goal-based, empirical theory," was the approach I chose to study ETV's implementation. This type of theory "expresses what is known about how to approach desired or desirable conditions."[2] Goal-based studies are a type of empirical theory supporting evaluation research generally. In this case study, I followed Reichardt and Cook's suggestion to use "qualitative and quantitative methods together" to evaluate ETV's implementation process and the results it produced.[3] The core research question was: Did Rock Hill's use of community-wide strategic planning as a tool to shape its future achieve some of the significant results promised by advocates of this tool? Eight sources of information were used in this stage:

(1) the author's tour of the city during a three-week site visit in September 1999;

(2) the RHEDC's newspaper clippings file, which contained over 1000 articles published between 1990 and 1999 in *The Herald*, Rock Hill's daily paper, and in the *Charlotte Observer-York Edition*;

(3) various municipal documents, such as annual reports, the city manager's budget messages, the mayor's annual State of the City speeches, city council minutes, numerous planning documents, and documents related to ETV's implementation and updating through the Empowering the Community (ETC) initiative, which took place in 1995;

(4) in-depth, structured interviews with 21 individuals serving in key leadership positions in city government and community organizations during the 1990s;

(5) questionnaires featuring six questions from the interview schedule that were completed by five Rock Hill leaders in lieu of in-depth interviews;

(6) the author's participation in the RHEDC's annual planning

retreat held October 31 - November 2, 1999 which featured a review of the ETV and ETC initiatives;
(7) numerous informal interviews with city officials and community leaders; and
(8) a survey mailed in Fall 1999 to 274 citizens who had worked on the six theme groups featured in ETV/ETC.

The survey consisted of ten statements about results one would expect to achieve in a successful community-wide strategic planning initiative. Theme group participants indicated the strength of their agreement or disagreement with each statement using a four point scale: 1 = "strongly disagree," 2 = "disagree," 3 = "agree" and 4 = "strongly agree." After two mailings, 113 theme group participants had returned a completed survey for a response rate of 41 percent. If the three citizens who were deceased and the 27 citizens who moved away from Rock Hill are excluded, then the adjusted response rate is 46 percent. Table A.1 displays the Gender and Race of all theme group participants and those participants who responded to the survey. Table A.2 displays the occupation and Table A.3 displays the party identification of theme group participants and those who responded to the survey. The data suggest that the 113 respondents are representative of the population of theme group participants, with only two exceptions: government employees and minorities who participated in the 1988 to 1989 planning process ("ETV Only") are under-represented.

Table A.1 Gender and Race of 124 ETV and 176 ETC Participants and the 113 ETV/ETC Participants Responding to Survey (Percentages Reported)

Initiative	N	Male	Female	White	Minority
ETV Only	98	73	27	86	14
Adjusted n	81	75	25	88	12
Responded	32	72	28	97	3
ETC Only	150	50	50	73	20
Adjusted n	137	50	50	74	19
Responded	62	53	47	82	18
ETV and ETC	26	65	35	85	15
Adjusted n	26	65	35	85	15
Responded	18	73	28	89	11

Notes: The initiative is not known for 1 respondent who is male, white, has a business occupation, and is a Republican. Data on race are missing for 10 ETC Only participants. "Adjusted n" refers to the number of citizens who are not known to have died or moved away from Rock Hill.

Table A.2 Occupation of 124 ETV and 176 ETC Participants and the
113 ETV/ETC Participants Responding to Survey
(Percentages Reported)

Initiative	N	Gov	Bus	Prof	Civic
ETV Only	98	9	34	49	6
Adjusted n	81	11	35	47	5
Responded	32	3	41	44	13
ETC Only	150	12	36	36	7
Adjusted n	137	12	36	36	6
Responded	62	10	37	50	32
ETV and ETC	26	12	38	35	15
Adjusted n	26	12	38	35	15
Responded	18	11	33	44	11

Notes: The initiative is not known for 1 respondent who is male, white, has a
business occupation, and is a Republican. Data on occupation are missing for 14
ETC Only participants and 2 ETV only participants are categorized as "other."
"Adjusted n" refers to the number of citizens who are not known to have died or
moved away from Rock Hill.

Table A.3 Political Party of 124 ETV and 176 ETC Participants and the
113 ETV/ETC Participants Responding to Survey
(Percentages Reported)

Initiative	N	Rep	Dem	Ind
ETV Only	98	NA	NA	NA
Adjusted n	81	NA	NA	NA
Responded	32	25	44	31
ETC Only	150	NA	NA	NA
Adjusted n	137	NA	NA	NA
Responded	62	32	34	29
ETV and ETC	26	NA	NA	NA
Adjusted n	26	NA	NA	NA
Responded	18	22	33	39

Notes: The initiative is not known for 1 respondent who is male, white, has a business occupation, and is a Republican. Data on political party are missing for 3 ETC Only participants and 1 ETV and ETC participant. Data on political party are not available (NA), except for survey respondents, because voters do not register by party in South Carolina. "Adjusted n" refers to the number of citizens who are not known to have died or moved away from Rock Hill.

Endnotes

Chapter 1 Community-Wide Strategic Planning and Urban Regime Theory

1. Theodore H. Poister and Gregory Streib, "Management Tools in Municipal Government: Trends Over the Past Decade," *Public Administration Review* 49, no. 3 (1989): 240-248.

2. John M. Bryson, *Strategic Planning for Public and Nonprofit Organizations*, Revised Edition (San Francisco: Jossey-Bass, 1995), 4-5.

3. Gerald L. Gordon, *Strategic Planning in Local Government* (Washington, DC: International City/County Management Association, 1993), 1.

4. U.S. Department of Commerce, *U.S. Census of Population 2000* (Washington, DC: Bureau of the Census, 2000).

5. Peter M. Judge, "Three Counties Tied Together in History," *The Herald*, 3 March 1989.

6. David R. Goldfield, "Urbanization in a Rural Culture," in *The South for New Southerners*, ed. Paul D. Escott and David R. Goldfield (Chapel Hill: The University of North Carolina Press, 1991), 76-77.

7. Peter M. Judge, "Three Counties Tied Together in History."

8. James C. Cobb, "The Sunbelt South: Industrialization in Regional, National, and International Perspective," in *Searching for the Sunbelt*, ed. Raymond A. Mohl (Knoxville: The University of Tennessee Press, 1990), 36.

9. David R. Goldfield and Blaine A. Brownell, *Urban America: A History*, Second Edition (Boston: Houghton Mifflin Company, 1990), 407.

10. Kenneth T. Jackson, *Crabgrass Frontier: The Suburbanization of the United States* (New York: Oxford University Press, 1985), 272.

11. David R. Goldfield, "The City as Southern History: The Past and The Promise of Tomorrow," in *The Future of the South: A Historical Perspective for the Twenty-first Century*, ed. Joe P. Dunn and Howard L. Preston (Urbana: University of Illinois Press, 1991), 39.

12. Goldfield, "The City as Southern History."

13. Goldfield, "The City as Southern History,' 37.

14. Betty Jo Rhea, Personal Communication. September 22, 1999; Russell Allen, Personal Communication. September 17, 1999.

15. Robert W. Rider, "Making Strategic Planning Work in Local

Government," *Long Range Planning* 16 (June 1983): 73-81; William M. Rohe and Lauren B. Gates, *Planning with Neighborhoods* (Chapel Hill: University of North Carolina Press, 1985); Donna L. Sorkin, Nancy B. Ferris, and James Hudak, *Strategies for Cities and Counties: A Strategic Planning Guide* (Washington, DC: Public Technology, Inc., 1984); Ronald L. Thomas, Mary C. Means, and Margaret Grieve, *Taking Charge: How Communities Are Planning Their Futures* (Washington, DC: International City Management Association, 1988).

16. John Stuart Hall and Louis F. Weschler, "The Phoenix Futures Forum: Creating Vision, Implanting Community," *National Civic Review* 80 (Spring 1990): 135-157; Bruce W. McClendon and John A. Lewis, "Goals for Corpus Christi: Citizen Participation in Planning," *National Civic Review* (February 1985): 72-80; Thomas, Means, and Grieve, *Taking Charge.*

17. Poister and Streib, "Management Tools in Municipal Government," 240-248.

18. Poister and Streib, "Management Tools in Municipal Government," 244.

19. Carmen Scavo, "The Use of Participative Mechanisms by Large American Cities," *Journal of Urban Affairs* 15 (1993): 93-109.

20. John M. Bryson and William D. Roering, "Initiation of Strategic Planning," *Public Administration Review* 48, no. 6 (1988): 995-1004.

21. Bryson and Roering, "Initiation of Strategic Planning," 1001-1002.

22. Sherry Chisenhall, "Secret of Success?," *The Charlotte Observer-York*, 16 February 1992, 1(Y) and 4(Y).

23. Gregory Streib and Theodore Poister, "The Use of Strategic Planning in Municipal Governments," in *The Municipal Year Book 2002*, (Washington, DC: International City/County Management Association, 2002), 18-25.

24. Streib and Poister, *The Municipal Year Book 2002*, 18-25.

25. Streib and Poister, *The Municipal Year Book 2002*, 18-25.

26. Gerry Stoker, "Regime Theory and Urban Politics," in *Theories of Urban Politics*, ed. David Judge, Gerry Stoker, and Harold Wolman (London: Sage Publications, 1995), 54.

27. Robert Pecorella, *Community Power in a Post Reform City* (Armonk, NY: M.E. Sharpe, 1994), 9.

28. Clarence N. Stone, *Regime Politics* (Lawrence, KS: University of Kansas Press, 1989), 6.

29. Stone, *Regime Politics*, 4.

30. Richard E. DeLeon, *Left Coast City* (Lawrence, KS: University of Kansas Press, 1992), 5-6.

31. Stone, *Regime Politics*, 9.

32. Pecorella, *Community Power in a Post Reform City*, 18.

33. Pecorella, *Community Power in a Post Reform City*, 24.

34. John Clayton Thomas, *Public Participation in Public Decisions*

(San Francisco: Jossey-Bass, 1995), 249.
    35. DeLeon, *Left Coast City*, 7-8.
    36. Clarence N. Stone, Marion E. Orr, and David Imbroscio, "The Reshaping of Urban Leadership in U.S. Cities: A Regime Analysis," in *Urban Life in Transition*, ed. M. Gottdiener and Chris G. Pickvance (Newbury Park: Sage Publications, 1991), 222-239.
    37. Stone, Orr, and Imbroscio, "The Reshaping of Urban Leadership," 227.
    38. Stone, Orr, and Imbroscio, "The Reshaping of Urban Leadership," 222-239.
    39. Stone, Orr, and Imbroscio, "The Reshaping of Urban Leadership," 235.
    40. Stone, Orr, and Imbroscio, "The Reshaping of Urban Leadership," 229.
    41. Stone, Orr, and Imbroscio, "The Reshaping of Urban Leadership," 230.
    42. Stone, Orr, and Imbroscio, "The Reshaping of Urban Leadership," 231.
    43. Stone, Orr, and Imbroscio, "The Reshaping of Urban Leadership," 231-232.
    44. Stone, Orr, and Imbroscio, "The Reshaping of Urban Leadership," 232.
    45. Stone, Orr, and Imbroscio, "The Reshaping of Urban Leadership," 233.
    46. Barbara Ferman, *Challenging the Growth Machine: Neighborhood Politics in Chicago and Pittsburgh* (Lawrence, KS: University of Kansas Press, 1996).
    47. Ferman, *Challenging the Growth Machine.*
    48. Ferman, *Challenging the Growth Machine*, 4.
    49. Ferman, *Challenging the Growth Machine*, 5.
    50. Ferman, *Challenging the Growth Machine*, 5.
    51. Ferman, *Challenging the Growth Machine*, 143.
    52. Ferman, *Challenging the Growth Machine.*
    53. Matthew Daly, "Rock Hill Chamber Reorganizes to Get 'Out Front," *The Charlotte Observer-York*, 16 December 1987, 1(B).
    54. Ferman, *Challenging the Growth Machine.*

Chapter 2 The Basic Design of Empowering the Vision

    1.   Douglas C. Eadie, "Putting a Powerful Tool to Practical Use: The Application of Strategic Planning in the Public Sector," *Public Administration Review* 43, no. 5 (1983): 447-52; Robert W. Rider, "Making Strategic Planning Work in Local Government," *Long Range Planning* 16 (June 1983): 73-81; Robert B. Denhardt, "Strategic Planning in State and Local

118 Endnotes

Government," *State and Local Government Review* 17, no. 1 (1985): 174-179; Ronald L. Thomas, Mary C. Means, and Margaret Grieve, *Taking Charge: How Communities Are Planning Their Futures* (Washington, DC: International City Management Association, 1988); Donna L. Sorkin, Nancy B. Ferris, and James Hudak, *Strategies for Cities and Counties: A Strategic Planning Guide* (Washington, DC: Public Technology, Inc., 1984).

2. Jerome L. Kaufman and Harvey M. Jacobs, "A Public Planning Perspective on Strategic Planning," *Journal of the American Planning Association* 53 (Winter 1987): 23-33.

3. John M. Bryson, *Strategic Planning for Public and NonProfit Organizations* (San Francisco: Jossey-Bass, 1988), 22-42.

4. Bryson, *Strategic Planning*, 48; Sorkin, Ferris, and Hudak, *Strategies for Cities and Counties*, 3.

5. Eadie, "Putting a Powerful Tool to Practical Use."

6. Eadie, "Putting a Powerful Tool to Practical Use," 247.

7. Kaufman and Jacobs, "A Public Planning Perspective," 29.

8. City of Rock Hill, *Theme Group Handbook* (1987).

9. City of Rock Hill, *Theme Group Handbook*.

10. City of Rock Hill, *Theme Group Handbook*, 2.

11. City of Rock Hill, *Theme Group Handbook*, 4.

12. Chris Handal, "Vision Farsighted, Officials Say," *The Herald*, 27 August 1988, 1(A) and 8(A).

13. Chris Handal, "Mayor Says All Citizens Can Have Say in Rock Hill's Future," *The Herald*, 8 March 1988, 1(A) and 10 (A).

14. Matthew Daly, "Preservation Key to Revitalization, Rock Hill Told," *The Charlotte Observer-York*, 13 May 1988, 1(A).

15. Chris Handal, "Older City Structures Surveyed," *The Herald*, 3 April 1988, 1(A) and 8(A).

16. Chris Handal, "To Work Magic, Take the Risk, Cultural Director Tells Group," *The Herald*, 27 July 1988, 1(A).

17. Chris Handal, "Architect to Speak on Plan for Paths Linking City's Parks," *The Herald*, 2 August 1988, 1(A).

18. Chris Handal, "Theater Consultant to Speak," *The Herald*, 10 August 1988, 6(A).

19. Chris Handal, "Offices Key to Downtown: Consultant," *The Herald*, 24 August 1988, 1(A).

20. City of Rock Hill, *Education Theme Group Final Report*, (1988).

21. Chris Handal, "Architect Unveils Downtown Plans," *The Herald*, 26 August 1988, 1(A) and 8(A).

22. Chris Handal, "Winthrop, Rock Hill Can Set Example for Nation: Dean," *The Herald*, 19 July 1988, 1(A).

23. Matthew Daly, "Rock Hill Studies Greenway," *The Charlotte Observer-York*, 20 July 1988, 1(Y).

24. City of Rock Hill, *Newsletter No. 3*, 1988.

25. City of Rock Hill, *Newsletter No. 2*, 1988.

26. City of Rock Hill, *Newsletter No. 3*.

27. Chris Handal, "Empowering the Vision Leaders Get Ready for Action," *The Herald*, 7 May 1989, 1(A).

28. Kim Gazella, "Rock Hill Shares Vision," *The Charlotte Observer-York*, 27 September 1989, 1(Y).

29. City of Rock Hill, *Theme Group Handbook*.

30. Handal, "Vision Farsighted, Officials Say," 1(A) and 8(A).

31. Richard V. Francaviglia, *Main Street Revisited* (Iowa City: The University of Iowa Press, 1996); Matthew Daly, "A Place for the 1990s' Plan Would Renew Downtown Rock Hill," *The Charlotte Observer-York*, 13 December 1987, 1(D) and 2(D).

32. Francaviglia, *Main Street Revisited*, 167.

33. City of Rock Hill, *Theme Group Handbook*.

34. Chris Handal, "Snapshots of the Future," *The Herald*, 23 March 1990, 1(A) and 8(A).

35. Chris Handal, "Resident's Ideas on City Plan Sought," *The Herald*, 3 September 1988, 1(A).

Chapter 3 Lessons from the Planning Process: 1987-1989

1. Bruce W. McClendon and John A. Lewis, "Goals for Corpus Christi: Citizen Participation in Planning," *National Civic Review* (February 1985): 72-80; Ronald L. Thomas, Mary C. Means, and Margaret Grieve, *Taking Charge: How Communities Are Planning Their Futures* (Washington, DC: International City Management Association, 1988); John Stuart Hall and Louis F. Weschler, "The Phoenix Futures Forum: Creating Vision, Implanting Community," *National Civic Review* 80 (Spring 1990): 135-157; Jason Woodmansee, 'Community Visioning: Citizen Participation in Strategic Planning," in *MIS Report* 26, no. 3 (Washington, DC: International City/County Management Association, 1994); Donald D. Chrislip and C.E. Larson, *Collaborative Leadership: How Citizens and Civic Leaders Can Make a Difference* (San Francisco: Jossey-Bass, 1994).

2. John M. Bryson, *Strategic Planning for Public and Nonprofit Organizations* (San Francisco: Jossey-Bass, 1988), 226.

3. John M. Bryson and William D. Roering, "Initiation of Strategic Planning," *Public Administration Review* 48, no. 6 (1988): 998.

4. Hall and Weschler, "The Phoenix Futures Forum," 138.

5. Donna L. Sorkin, Nancy B. Ferris, and James Hudak, *Strategies for Cities and Counties: A Strategic Planning Guide* (Washington, DC: Public Technology, Inc., 1984), 14.

6. James H. Svara, *Official Leadership in the City* (New York: Oxford University Press, 1990); Craig M. Wheeland, "A Profile of a Facilitative Mayor: Mayor Betty Jo Rhea of Rock Hill, SC," in *Facilitative*

Leadership in Local Government, ed. James H. Svara (San Francisco: Sage Publications, 1994), 136-159.

7.   Sorkin, Ferris, and Hudak, *Strategies for Cities and Counties*, 12; Hall and Weschler, "The Phoenix Futures Forum," 153.

8.   Sorkin, Ferris, and Hudak, *Strategies for Cities and Counties*, 12.

9.   Bryson, *Strategic Planning*, 64; Sorkin, Ferris, and Hudak, *Strategies for Cities and Counties*, 20; Thomas, Means, and Grieve, *Taking Charge*, 14.

10.   Sorkin, Ferris, and Hudak, *Strategies for Cities and Counties*, 38; Bryson and Roering, "Initiation of Stategic Planning," 1000; Bryson, *Strategic Planning*, 226; Hall and Weschler, "The Phoenix Future Forum," 138 and 156.

11.   Sorkin, Ferris, and Hudak, *Strategies for Cities and Counties*, 38.

12.   Bryson and Roering, "Initiation of Strategic Planning," 1000.

13.   Bryson and Roering, "Initiation of Strategic Planning," 1000.

14.   Bryson and Roering, "Initiation of Strategic Planning," 1000.

15.   Bryson, *Strategic Planning*; Sorkin, Ferris, and Hudak, *Strategies for Cities and Counties*; Thomas, Means, and Grieve, *Taking Charge*.

16.   Bryson, *Strategic Planning*, 228.

17.   Matthew Daly, "Preservation Key to Revitalization, Rock Hill Told," *The Charlotte Observer-York*, 13 May 1988, 1(A); Chris Handal, "Older City Structures Surveyed," *The Herald*, 3 April 1988, 1(A) and 8(A); Chris Handal, "To Work Magic, Take the Risk, Cultural Director Tells Group," *The Herald*, 27 July 1988, 1(A); Chris Handal, "Architect to Speak on Plan for Paths Linking City's Parks," *The Herald*, 2 August 1988, 1(A); Chris Handal, "Theater Consultant to Speak," *The Herald*, 10 August 1988, 6(A); Chris Handal, "Offices Key to Downtown: Consultant," *The Herald*, 24 August 1988, 1(A).

18.   Sorkin, Ferris, and Hudak, *Strategies for Cities and Counties*, 14-15.

19.   Camille Cates, "Beyond Muddling: Creativity," *Public Administration Review* 48 (November/December 1979): 527-532.

20.   Bryson, *Strategic Planning*, 181; Robert B. Denhardt, "Strategic Planning in State and Local Government," *State and Local Government Review* 17, no. 1 (1985): 177; Sorkin, Ferris, and Hudak, *Strategies for Cities and Counties*, 46.

21.   Chris Handal, "Vision Farsighted, Officials Say," *The Herald*, 27 August 1988, 1(A) and 8(A).

22.   Joe Lanford, Persona Communication. 1990.

23.   Thomas, Means, and Grieve, *Taking Charge*, 33.

24.   Bryson, *Strategic Planning*, 193.

25.   Lanford, Personal Communication. 1990.

26. Chris Handal, "Snapshots of the Future," *The Herald*, 23 March 1990, 1(A) and 8(A).

27. Denhardt, "Strategic Planning in State and Local Government," 176; Bryson, *Strategic Planning*, 208; Thomas, Means, and Grieve, *Taking Charge*, 13-14; Sorken, Ferris, and Hudak, *Strategies for Cities and Counties*, 19; McClendon and Lewis, "Goals for Corpus Christi," 79; William R. Potapchuk, "New Approaches to Citizen Participation: Building Consent," *National Civic Review* 80 (Spring 1990): 165.

28. Sorkin, Ferris, and Hudak, *Strategies for Cities and Counties*; Potapchuk, "New Approaches," 158-168.

29. William M. Rohe and Lauren B. Gates, *Planning with Neighborhoods* (Chapel Hill: University of North Carolina Press, 1985), 75; Sorkin, Ferris, and Hudak, *Strategies for Cities and Counties*, 38; Paul E. Peterson, "Forms of Representation: Participation of the Poor in the Community Action Program," *American Political Science Review* 64 (June 1970): 494-495.

30. Hannah Pitkin, *The Concept of Representation* (Berkeley: University of California Press, 1967).

31. Edward C. Banfield and James Q. Wilson, *City Politics* (New York: Random House, 1963); James Q. Wilson, "Planning and Politics: Citizen Participation in Urban Renewal," in *Urban Renewal: The Record and the Controversy*, ed. James Q. Wilson (Cambridge: M.I.T. Press, 1966), 407-421.

32. U.S. Department of Commerce, *U.S. Census of Population 1980* (Washington, DC: Bureau of the Census, 1980)

33. Rohe and Gates, *Planning with Neighborhoods*, 191; Sy Adler and Gerald F. Blake, "The Effects of a Formal Citizen Participation Program on Involvement in the Planning Process: A Case Study of Portland, Oregon," *State and Local Government Review* (Winter 1990): 37-43; Thomas, Means, and Grieve, *Taking Charge*; Christine M. Reed, B.J. Reed, and Jeffrey S. Luke, "Assessing Readiness for Economic Development Strategic Planning," *Journal of the American Planning Association* 53 (Autumn 1987): 524; Barry Checkoway, "Two Types of Planning in Neighborhoods," *Journal of Planning Education and Research* 3 (1984): 102-109; Barry Checkoway, "The Irony of Neighborhood Planning," *National Civic Review* 79 (November/December 1990): 552-560.

34. Sorkin, Ferris, and Hudak, *Strategies for Cities and Counties*, 52; Douglas C. Eadie, "Putting a Powerful Tool to Practical Use: The Application of Strategic Planning in the Public Sector," *Public Administration Review* 43, no. 5 (1983): 449; Robert W. Rider, "Making Strategic Planning Work in Local Government," *Long Range Planning* 16 (June 1983): 77.

35. Lanford, Personal Communication. 1990.

36. Ken Garfield, "Haves Help the Have-Nots Empower Their Own Vision," *The Charlotte Observer-York*, 13 July 1990, 1(Y).

37. Chris Handal, "Council to Review Spending Proposal," *The Herald*, 21 July 1990, 4(A); Chris Handal, "City Council to Consider Higher

Wrecker Fee," *The Herald*, 11 August 1990, 4(A).
        38. City of Rock Hill, *Comment Log*, 1989.

Chapter 4 Achieving the Vision: ETV Ten Years Later

        1. Gerald L. Gordon, *Strategic Planning in Local Government*
(Washington, DC: International City/County Management Association, 1993),
3.
        2. Donna L. Sorkin, Nancy B. Ferris, and James Hudak, *Strategies
for Cities and Counties: A Strategic Planning Guide* (Washington, DC: Public
Technology, Inc., 1984); Ronald L. Thomas, Mary C. Means, and Margaret
Grieve, *Taking Charge: How Communities Are Planning Their Futures*
(Washington, DC: International City Management Association, 1988); Gordon,
Strategic Planning in Local Government; John M. Bryson, *Strategic Planning
for Public and Nonprofit Organizations*, Revised Edition. (San Francisco:
Jossey-Bass, 1995); Derek Okubo, *The Community Visioning and Strategic
Planning Handbook* (Denver, CO: The National Civic League Press, 1997), 5:
Jason Woodmansee, "Community Visioning: Citizen Participation in Strategic
Planning," in *MIS Report* 26, no. 3 (Washington, DC: International
City/County Management Association, 1994), 1-2.
        3. Sorkin, Ferris, and Hudak, *Strategies for Cities and Counties*, 52.
        4. Sorkin, Ferris, and Hudak, *Strategies for Cities and Counties*, 52;
Okubo, *The Community Visioning and Strategic Planning Handbook*, 37.
        5. Betty Jo Rhea, Personal Communication. September 22, 1999;
Joe Lanford, Personal Communication. September 20, 1999; Doug Echols,
Personal Communication. September 21,1999; Russell Allen, Personal
Communication. September 21, 1999.
        6. Rhea, Personal Communication. September 22,1999; Allen,
Personal Communication. September 17, 1999.
        7. Broach, Mijeski, & Associates, *Quality of Services Survey* (City
of Rock Hill, SC, 1987); Broach, Mijeski, & Associates, *Business/City Survey*
(City of Rock Hill, SC, 1988); Broach, Mijeski, & Associates, *Needs
Assessment Survey* (City of Rock Hill, SC, 1994); Broach, Mijeski, &
Associates, *Budget Survey* (City of Rock Hill, SC, 1997).
        8. Broach, Mijeski, & Associates, *The Downtown Area Study* (Rock
Hill Chamber of Commerce, 1992).
        9. Judy H. Longshaw, "Further Study Ordered for Downtown Plan,"
The Herald, 19 March 1996; Judy H. Longshaw, "Group Taking Notes About
City's Future," *The Herald*, 15 August 1996.
        10. Participants were asked to indicate the strength of their agreement
with each of the ten statements using a four-point scale: 1 = strongly disagree, 2
= disagree, 3 = agree, and 4 = strongly agree. I interpret means above 2.5
indicating some agreement with the statement and scores below 2.5 as
indicating some disagreement. This is a subjective judgment that I argue is

reasonable in light of the limitations of using a four-point scale, rather than a five-point scale. By using the 2.5 midpoint, I avoid setting up a standard that will understate disagreement (using 2) or understate agreement (using three). I also use the same rationale when interpreting the data from four-point scales in Table 4.4. In a five-point scale I would use 3.0 as the mid-point. Note that for all ten statements in Table 4.2 the median is three which indicates "agreement."

     11. Sorkin, Ferris, and Hudak, *Strategies for Cities and Counties*; William R. Potapchuk, "Building an Infrastructure of Community Collaboration," *National Civic Review* 88, no. 3 (1999): 165-169; Donald D. Chrislip and C.E. Larson, *Collaborative Leadership: How Citizens and Civic Leaders Can Make a Difference* (San Francisco: Jossey-Bass, 1994); Thomas, Means, and Grieve, *Taking Charge*; Arthur T. Himmelman, "Communities Working Collaboratively for a Change," in *Resolving Conflict: Strategies for Local Government*, ed. Margaret S. Herrman (Washington, DC: International City/County Management Association, 1994), 27-29; Beverly A. Cigler, "Adjusting to Changing Expectations at the Local Level," in *Handbook of Public Administration*, 2nd Edition, ed. James L. Perry (San Francisco: Jossey-Bass, 1996).

     12. Chrislip and Larson, *Collaborative Leadership*, 5; See also Donna J. Wood and Barbara Gray, "Toward a Comprehensive Theory of Collaboration," *Journal of Applied Behavioral Science* 27, no. 2 (1991): 146-149, for a careful discussion of the concept.

     13. Okubo, *The Community Visioning and Strategic Planning Handbook*, 6; William R. Potapchuk, Jarle P. Crocker, and William H. Schechter, "The Transformative Power of Governance," *National Civic Review* 88, no. 3, (1999): 220-221; Susan Carpenter, "Solving Community Problems by Consensus," in *Resolving Conflict: Strategies for Local Government*, ed. Margaret S. Herrman (Washington, DC: International City/County Management Association, 1994), 138; Mary Walsh, *Building Citizen Involvement: Strategies for Local Government* (Washington, DC: International City/County Management Association, 1997), 93-102; See Judith E. Innes, "Planning through Consensus Building: A New View of the Comprehensive Planning Ideal," *Journal of the American Planning Association* 62, no. 4 (1996): 460-473, on consensus building as a tool in traditional comprehensive planning.

     14. Amy Helling, "Collaborative Visioning: Proceed with Caution!: Results from Evaluating Atlanta's Vision 2020 Project," *Journal of the American Planning Association* 64, no. 3 (1998): 335-340; Sue R. Faerman, "Managing Conflicts Creatively," in *Handbook of Public Administration*, 2nd Edition, ed. James L. Perry (San Francisco: Jossey-Bass, 1996), 636-637; John Parr and David Lampe, "Empowering Citizens," in *Handbook of Public Administration*, 2nd Edition, ed. James L. Perry (San Francisco: Jossey-Bass, 1996), 204.

     15. Sorkin, Ferris, and Hudak, *Strategies for Cities and Counties*, 50.

16. City of Rock Hill, *Minutes to City Council Meeting*, 13 November 1989.

17. Broach, Mijeski, & Associates, *Quality of Services Survey*; Broach, Mijeski, & Associates, *Business/City Survey*; Broach, Mijeski, & Associates, *The Downtown Area Study*; Broach, Mijeski, & Associates, *Needs Assessment Survey*; Broach, Mijeski, & Associates, *Budget Survey*; Palmetto Benchmarking Project, *Survey Results for the City of Rock Hill* (Columbia, SC: Institute of Public Affairs, University of South Carolina, 1998).

18. Thomas, Means, and Grieve, *Taking Charge*; Chrislip and Larson, *Collaborative Leadership*; Woodmansee, "Community Visioning;" Okubo, *The Community Visioning and Strategic Planning Handbook*.

19. Walsh, *Building Citizen Involvement*, 41.

20. Michael K. Briand, *Building Deliberative Communities* (Charlottesville, VA: Pew Partnership for Civic Change, 1995), 11.

21. Richard C. Box, *Citizen Governance: Leading American Communities into the 21st Century* (Thousand Oaks, CA: Sage Publications, 1998) 82.

22. Jeffrey Berry, Kent Portney, and Ken Thomson, *The Rebirth of Urban Democracy* (Washington, DC: Brookings Institution, 1993).

23. Berry, Portney, and Thomson, *The Rebirth of Urban Democracy*.

24. Berry, Portney, and Thomson, *The Rebirth of Urban Democracy*, 54-55.

25. Berry, Portney, and Thomson, *The Rebirth of Urban Democracy*, 55.

26. Berry, Portney, and Thomson, *The Rebirth of Urban Democracy*, 55.

27. Berry, Portney, and Thomson, *The Rebirth of Urban Democracy*, 55.

28. John Clayton Thomas, *Public Participation in Public Decisions* (San Francisco: Jossey-Bass, 1995), 56.

29. See John M. Bryson and William D. Roering, "Initiation of Strategic Planning," *Public Administration Review* 48, no. 6 (1988): 995-1004 for a discussion of the different conceptions of time used by participants in strategic planning processes.

30. Thomas, Means, and Grieve, *Taking Charge*, 13-14.

31. Bryson, *Strategic Planning for Public and Nonprofit Organizations*, 166.

32. Chrislip and Larson, *Collaborative Leadership*, 107.

33. Chrislip and Larson, *Collaborative Leadership*, 53-54: Evan Berman, "Dealing with Cynical Citizens," *Public Administration Review* 57, no. 2 (1997): 110; Edmund C. Weeks, "The Practice of Deliberative Democracy: Results from Four Large-Scale Trials," *Public Administration Review* 60, no. 4 (2000): 360-372; See Robert D. Putnam, "Bowling Alone: America's Declining Social Capital," *Journal of Democracy* 6, no. 1 (1995): 67, for a discussion of social capital.

34. Chris Handal, "School Board's Decision Affects Downtown Plan," *The Herald*, 30 October 1991, 5(A).

35. Chris Handal, "Council OKs Bed-Tax Guidelines, 16.2 Million Bond Issue," *The Herald*, 24 July 1990, 4(A).

36. Andrea K. Walker, "Chamber Chief Foresees a Rock Hill Explosion as Growth Continues," *Charlotte Observer-York Edition*, 2 January 1999, 1(Y) and 3(Y).

37. City of Rock Hill, *City Manager's 1999 Budget Message*, 30 December 1998.

38. Melanie Brandon, Personal Communication. September 28, 1999.

39. Dennis Merrell, Personal Communication. September 23, 1999.

40. Michael McGuire, Barry Rubin, Robert Agranoff, and Craig Richards, "Building Development Capacity in NonMetropolitan Communities," *Public Administration Review* 54, no.5 (1994): 431.

41. William R. Potapchuk, Jarle P. Crocker, Dina Boogaard, and William H. Schechter, *Building Community: Exploring the Role of Social Capital and Local Government* (Washington, DC: Program for Community Problem Solving, 1998), 10.

42. National Civic League, *The Civic Index* (Denver, CO: The National Civic League Press, 1999), 13.

43. Karen M. Hult and Charles Walcott, *Governing Public Organizations: Politics, Structures, and Institutional Design* (Pacific Grove, CA: Brooks/Cole Publishing, 1990), 97.

44. See Beverly A. Ciglar, "Pre-Conditions for the Emergence of Multicommunity Collaborative Organizations," *Policy Studies Review* 16, no. 1 (1999): 88-89, on types of Partnerships.

45. Sorkin, Ferris, and Hudak, *Strategies for Cities and Counties*, 51; See also Bryson, *Strategic Planning for Public and Nonprofit Organizations*, 170; Bruce W. McClendon and John A. Lewis, "Goals for Corpus Christi: Citizen Participation in Planning," *National Civic Review* (February 1985): 79.

Chapter 5 Political Factions and Regime Formation

1. Clarence N. Stone, Marion E. Orr, and David Imbroscio, "The Reshaping of Urban Leadership in U.S. Cities: A Regime Analysis," in *Urban Life in Transition*, ed. M. Gottdiener and Chris G. Pickvance (Newbury Park: Sage Publications, 1991), 227.

2. Stone, Orr, and Imbrocsio, "The Reshaping of Urban Leadership," 227.

3. James H. Svara and Associates, *Facilitative Leadership in Local Government* (San Francisco: Jossey-Bass Publishers, 1994).

4. James H. Svara, *Official Leadership in the City* (New York:

Oxford University Press, 1990), 82.

5.   Svara, "Mayors in the Unity of Powers Context: Effective
Leadership in Council-Manager Governments," in *The Future of Local
Government Administration*, eds. H. George Frederickson and John Nalbandian
(Washington, DC: International City/County Management Association, 2002),
47.

6.   Svara, *Facilitative Leadership in Local Government*, 16.

7.   Svara, *Facilitative Leadership in Local Government*; Glen W.
Sparrow, "The Emerging Chief Executive 1971-1991: A San Diego Update," in
Facilitative Leadership in Local Government, ed. James H. Svara (San
Francisco: Sage Publication, 1994), 187-199.

8.   Lou Parris, "Jerome Stays In: Gill, Berry Out," *The Herald*, 21
October 1981, 1 and 3.

9.   Svara, *Facilitative Leadership in Local Government*.

10.   Craig M. Wheeland, "A Profile of a Facilitative Mayor: Mayor
Betty Jo Rhea of Rock Hill, SC," in *Facilitative Leadership in Local
Government*, ed. James H. Svara (San Francisco: Sage Publications, 1994),
136-159.

11.   Svara, *Facilitative Leadership in Local Government*, 16.

12.   Doug Echols, Personal Communication. September 21, 1999.

13.   Betty Jo Rhea, Personal Communication. September 22, 1999.

14.   Echols, Personal Communication. September 21, 1999.

15.   Echols, Personal Communication. September 21, 1999.

16.   Andrea K. Walker, "Vision Unveiled for City of Dreams,"
Charlotte Observer-York Edition, 27 May 1998, 1(Y) and 3(Y).

17.   Don Harper, "RHEDC Embarks on Tenth Year," *The Herald*,
30 January 1992.

18.   Wheeland, "A Profile of a Facilitative Mayor," 136-159.

19.   Jim Morrill, "Two Blacks Win Council Primary," *The Herald*,
17 October 1979, 1; Sula S. Pettibon, "Rhea Wins Mayoral Primary," *The
Herald*, 16 October 1985, 1 and 18; Justine McGuire, "Incumbents Gill, Sutton
Re-elected," *The Herald*, 20 October 1999, 1.

20.   City of Rock Hill, *Minutes to City Council Meeting*, 4 May
1993.

21.   Judy H. Longshaw, "Council Narrowly OKs Grant for Park,"
The Herald, 15 November 1994, 1.

22.   Andrea K. Walker, "Sutton and Echols Unleash Attack Ads,"
Charlotte Observer-York Edition, 31 October 1997, 1(Y) and 4(Y).

23.   City of Rock Hill, *Minutes to City Council Meeting*, 14
December 1998.

24.   Chris Handal and Cal Harrison, "Schools, County Seek Galleria
Tax," *The Herald*, 16 August 1991, 1(A).

25.   Handal and Harrison, "Schools, County Seek Galleria Tax,"
1(A).

26.   Staff Reports, "School Board Rejects Galleria Tax District," *The*

Herald, 30 August 1991, 1(A).
    27. Mark Price, "Schools Accept Tax Deal," *Charlotte Observer-York Edition*, 6 September 1991, 1(Y).
    28. Price, "Schools Accept Tax Deal," 1(Y).
    29. City of Rock Hill, *Minutes to City Council Meeting*, 14 December 1998.
    30. David Milstead, "County Files Suit Against Rock Hill," *The Herald*, 2 January 1999, A1.
    31. Chad Simpson, "City, County Settle Suit," *The Herald*, 29 July 1999, 1(A).
    32. Broach, Mijeski, & Associates, *Quality of Service Survey* (City of Rock Hill, SC, 1987): 1.
    33. Broach, Mijeski, & Associates, *Business/City Survey* (City of Rock Hill, SC, 1988): 1.
    34. Broach, Mijeski, & Associates, *The Downtown Area Study* (Rock Hill Chamber of Commerce, 1992).:2
    35. Broach, Mijeski, & Associates, *Needs Assessment Survey* (City of Rock Hill, SC, 1994):1.
    36. Palmetto Benchmarking Project, *Survey Results for the City of Rock Hill* (Columbia, SC: Institute of Public Affairs, University of South Carolina, 1998): Table 2.
    37. Broach, Mijeski, & Associates, *Quality of Service Survey*; Broach, Mijeski, & Associates, *Needs Assessment Survey*; Broach, Mijeski, & Associates, *Budget Survey* (City of Rock Hill, SC, 1997): Table 4.
    38. See Nicole Gustin, "City in Debt $89 Million," *The Herald*, 21 September 1997, 1; Andrea K. Walker, "In Rock Hill Mayor's Race, Money's the Main Issue," *Charlotte Observer-York Edition*, 2 November 1997, 1(Y) and 5(Y); Jen Pilla, "Social Advocate Gill Files for Full Term on Council," *Charlotte Observer-York Edition*, 27 July 1999, 1(Y) and 3(Y); Jen Pilla, "Sutton Files to Keep Seat on Rock Hill City Council," *Charlotte Observer-York Edition*, 27 July 1999, 1(Y) and 3(Y); Justin McGuire, "Rock Hill Councilwoman Defends Ward Seat," *The Herald*, 12 October 1999, 1.
    39. Al Dozier, "Campaign Ads Strike Nerve," *The Herald*, 31 October 1997, 1; Walker, "In Rock Hill Mayor's Race, Money's the Main Issue," 1(Y) and 5(Y).
    40. City of Rock Hill, *Minutes to City Council Meeting*, 25 April 1994.
    41. Parris, "Jerome Stays In," 1 and 3; Pettibon, "Rhea Wins Mayoral Primary," 1 and 18.
    42. Kevin Sutton, Personal Communication. September 21, 1999.
    43. City of Rock Hill, *Minutes to City Council Meeting*, 25 April 1994.
    44. Jason Cato, "Rock Hill Mayoral Candidates Tout Backgrounds, Experience at Forum," *The Herald*, 3 October 2001, 1(A).

Chapter 6 Conflict, Cooperation and Issue-Based Politics

1. Craig M. Wheeland, "Citywide Strategic Planning: An Evaluation of Rock Hill's Empowering the Vision," *Public Administration Review* 53, no. 1 (1993): 65-72.

2. Wheeland, "Citywide Strategic Planning," 65-72; Winston Searles, Personal Communication. September 22, 1999; Osbey Roddey, Personal Communication. September 29, 1999..

3. Rufus P. Browning, Dale Rogers Marshall, and David H. Tabb, *Racial Politics in American Cities* (New York: Longman, 1997), 9.

4. Matthew Daly, "Rock Hill's Next Step: Sell District Plan to Voters," *The Charlotte Observer-York*, 11 September 1988, 1.

5. Daly, "Rock Hill's Next Step," 1.

6. Chris Handal, "Single-Member Districts Approved," *The Herald*, 26 April 1989, 1(A).

7. Andrea K. Walker, "City Envisions Saluda Street Revival," *Charlotte Observer-York Edition*, 8 January 1999, 1(Y) and 3(Y).

8. Chris Handal, "Vision Farsighted, Officials Say," The Herald, 27 August 1988, 8(A).

9. Chris Handal, "Vision Leaders Pledge Commitment," *The Herald*, 14 May 1989, 9(A).

10. Chris Handal, "As Gateway Rises, So Do Visions of New City," *The Herald*, 30 September 1990, 1(A) and 14(A).

11. Handal, "As Gateway Rises," 1(A) and 14(A).

12. Doug Mauldin, "Price for Gateway, Civitas at Least $1.27 Million, Official Says," *The Herald*, 17 April 1991.

13. Doug Mauldin, "Rock Hill to Get Star Treatment," *The Herald*, 13 July 1996; Jennifer Becknell, "Arts Center Coming to Life," *The Herald*, 18 February 1996, 2(C).

14. Doug Most, "Spratt, Arts Council Can Keep Offices," *The Herald*, 9 February 1993.

15. Doug Mauldin, "City Rejects Petitions for Bond Referendum," *The Herald*, 19 November 1992.

16. Joe Lanford, Personal Communication. September 20, 1999.

17. Lanford, Personal Communication. September 20, 1999.

18. Maxine Gill, Personal Communication. September 21, 1999.

19. Mauldin, "City Rejects Petitions."

20. Kim Gazella, "Council Agrees to Let Architect Aid Rock Hill's Renovation," *The Charlotte Observer-York*, 10 April 1990.

21. Gazella, "Council Agrees," 34(Y).

22. Rock Hill Economic Development Corporation, *Annual Report*, 1991.

23. Sally White, "Skeptical About Downtown Plan," *The Herald*, 29

May 1989.

24. Chris Handal, "Downtown 'Vision' Tab: $11 Million," *The Herald*, 27 May 1990, 1(A) and 14(A); Editorial, "Does the Private Sector Share Planners' Vision?," *The Herald*, 29 May 1990, 6(A).

25. Sherry Chisenhall, "Secret of Success?," *The Charlotte Observer-York*, 16 February 1992, 1(Y) and 4(Y).

26. Chisenhall, "Secret of Success?," 1(Y) and 4(Y).

27. Doug Mauldin, "Developer Fears Park Will Boost Rates," *The Herald*, 29 March 1992, 10(A).

28. Mauldin, "Developer Fears," 10(A).

29. Susan McKenzie, "Turner's Vision Tied to City's Past," *The Herald*, 25 October 1993, 6(B).

30. McKenzie, "Turner's Vision," 6(B).

31. Ken Elkins, "Development Director Says City-Funded Study 'Politically Motivated'," *The Herald*, 16 November 1995.

32. Clay Andrews, Personal Communication. September 28, 1999.

33. Susan Hill, "City: Accountant's Suggestions Nothing New," *The Herald*, 11 October 1994.

34. City of Rock Hill, *Minutes to City Council Meeting*, 14 December 1992.

35. Susan Hill, "Businesses Charged Up Over City's Power Rates," *The Herald*, 14 June 1994, 1(A).

36. Hill, "City: Accountant's Suggestions Nothing New."

37. Hill, "City: Accountant's Suggestions Nothing New."

38. Hill, "City: Accountant's Suggestions Nothing New."

39. Cal Harrison, "Analysts Credit NCMPA's Rating to Growth, Management," *The Herald*, 31 July 1995.

40. Judy H. Longshaw, "City Tries to Wean Self from Utility," *The Herald*, 11 November 1995.

41. Patrick Scott, "1995 Rock Hill Passes Its Fiscal Exam," *The Charlotte Observer-York*, 30 October 1995, 1(Y) and 3(Y).

42. Judy H. Longshaw, "Further Study Ordered for Downtown Plan," *The Herald*, 19 March 1996; Judy H. Longshaw, "Group Taking Notes About City's Future," *The Herald*, 15 August 1996.

43. Longshaw, "Group Taking Notes."

44. City of Rock Hill, *City Manager's 1999 Budget Message*, 30 December 1998.

45. City of Rock Hill, *City Manager's 1999 Budget Message*.

46. Robert Pecorella, *Community Power in a Post Reform City* (Armonk, NY: M.E. Sharpe, 1994).

47. City of Rock Hill, *Minutes to City Council Meeting*, 13 November 1989.

48. Justin McGuire, "Rock Hill Councilwoman Defends Ward Seat," *The Herald*, 12 October 1999, 1.

49. Gill, Personal Communication. September 21, 1999.

50. Gill, Personal Communication. September 21, 1999.
51. Gill, Personal Communication. September 21, 1999.
52. Judy H. Longshaw, "3 Seats Up for Vote," *The Herald*, 15 October 1995.
53. Longshaw, "3 Seats Up for Vote."
54. Longshaw, "3 Seats Up for Vote."
55. Searles, 1999. Interview by author.
56. Chad Simpson, "City, County Settle Suit," *The Herald*, 29 July 1999, 1(A).
57. Justin McGuire, "Incumbents Gill, Sutton Re-elected," *The Herald*, 20 October 1999, 1.
58. Searles, Personal Communication. September 22, 1999..

Chapter 7 Using Community-Wide Strategic Planning in the Future

1. Barbara C. Crosby, "Leading in a Shared-Power World," in *Handbook of Public Administration*, 2nd Edition, ed. James L. Perry (San Francisco, Jossey-Bass, 1996), 619.
2. Crosby, "Leading in a Shared-Power World," 619.
3. Clarence N. Stone, Marion E. Orr, and David Imbroscio, "The Reshaping of Urban Leadership in U.S. Cities: A Regime Analysis," in *Urban Life in Transition*, ed. M. Gottdiener and Chris G. Pickvance (Newbury Park: Sage Publications, 1991), 222-239.
4. Jason Cato, "A Vision Started the Ball Rolling on Redevelopment," *The Herald*, 16 April 2002, 13(G).
5. Barbara Ferman, *Challenging the Growth Machine: Neighborhood Politics in Chicago and Pittsburgh* (Lawrence, KS: University of Kansas Press, 1996).

Appendix Research Design

1. Robert T. Golembiewski, "The Future of Public Administration: End of a Short Stay in the Sun? Or a New Day A-Dawning," *Public Administration Review* 56, no. 2 (1996): 139-148.
2. Golembiewski, "The Future of Public Administration," 144.
3. Charles S. Reichardt and Thomas D. Cook, "Beyond Qualitative Versus Quantitative Methods," in *Qualitative and Quantitative Methods in Evaluation Research*, ed. T. Cook and C. Reichardt (Beverly Hills, CA: Sage Publications, 1979), 19.

Bibliography

Adler, Sy and Gerald F. Blake. "The Effects of a Formal Citizen
    Participation Program on Involvement in the Planning Process:
    A Case Study of Portland, Oregon." *State and Local
    Government Review* 22, no.1 (Winter 1990): 37-43.
Allen, Russell. Personal Communication. September 17, 1999.
Andrews, Clay. Personal Communication. September 28, 1999.
Becknell, Jennifer. "Arts Center Coming to Life." *The Herald*, 18
    February, 1996: 2C.
Banfield, Edward C. and James Q. Wilson. *City Politics*. New York:
    Random House, 1963.
Berman, Evan. "Dealing With Cynical Citizens." *Public Administration
    Review* 57, no.2 (March April 1997): 105-112.
Berry, Jeffrey, Kent Portney and Ken Thompson. *The Rebirth of Urban
    Democracy*. Washington, DC: Brookings Institution, 1993.
Box, Richard C. *Citizen Governance: Leading American Communities
    into the 21st Century*. Thousand Oaks, CA: Sage Publications,
    1998.
Brandon, Melanie. Personal Communication. September 28, 1999.
Briand, Michael K. *Building Deliberative Communities*. Charlottesville,
    VA: Pew Partnership for Civic Change, 1995.
Broach, Mijeski, & Associates. *Quality of Services Survey*. Rock Hill,
    SC.: City of Rock Hill, 1987
    _____. *Business/City Survey*. Rock Hill, SC.: City of Rock Hill,
    1988.
    _____. *The Downtown Area Study*. Rock Hill, SC.: Rock Hill
    Chamber of Commerce, 1992.
    _____. *Needs Assessment Survey*. Rock Hill, SC.: City of Rock
    Hill, 1994.
    _____. *Budget Survey*. Rock Hill, SC.: City of Rock Hill, 1997.
Browning, Rufus P., Dale Rogers Marshall, and David H. Tabb. *Racial
    Politics in American Cities*. New York: Longman, 1997.
Bryson, John M. *Strategic Planning for Public and NonProfit
    Organizations*. Revised Edition. San Francisco: Jossey-Bass,

1995.

_____. *Strategic Planning for Public and NonProfit Organizations.*
San Francisco: Jossey-Bass, 1988.

_____. and William D. Roering. "Initiation of Strategic Planning."
Public Administration Review 48, no. 6 (November/December
1988): 995-1004.

Cates, Camille. "Beyond Muddling: Creativity." *Public Administration
Review* 39, no. 6 (November/December 1979): 527-532.

Cato, Jason. "Rock Hill Mayoral Candidates Tout Backgrounds,
Experience at Forum." *The Herald,* 3 October 2001: 1A.

_____. "A Vision Started the Ball Rolling on Redevelopment." *The
Herald,* 16 April 2002: 13G.

Carpenter, Susan. "Solving Community Problems by Consensus." Pp.
137-147 in *Resolving Conflict: Strategies for Local
Government,* edited by Margaret S. Herrman. Washington,
DC: International City/County Management Association,
1994.

Checkoway, Barry. "The Irony of Neighborhood Planning." *National
Civic Review* 79 (November/December 1990): 552-560.

_____. "Two Types of Planning in Neighborhoods." *Journal of
Planning Education and Research* 3 (1984): 102-109.

Chisenhall, Sherry. "Secret of Success?" *The Charlotte Observer-
York,* 16 February 1992: 1Y, 4Y.

_____. "U.S. Mayors Honor Rock Hill for Planning, Livability."
The Charlotte Observer-York, 21 June 1992.

Chrislip, Donald D., and C. E. Larson. *Collaborative Leadership: How
Citizens and Civic Leaders Can Make a Difference.* San
Francisco: Jossey-Bass, 1994.

Cigler, Beverly A. "Adjusting to Changing Expectations at the Local
Level." Pp. 60-76 in *Handbook of Public Administration.* 2nd
ed. edited by James L. Perry. San Francisco: Jossey-Bass,
1996.

_____. "Pre-Conditions for the Emergence of Multicommunity
Collaborative Organizations." *Policy Studies Review* 16, no.
1(1999): 86-102.

Cobb, James C. "The Sunbelt South: Industrialization in Regional,
National, and International Perspective." Pp. 25-46 in
Searching for the Sunbelt. Edited by Raymond A. Mohl.
Knoxville: The University of Tennessee Press, 1990.

City of Rock Hill. *Theme Group Handbook.* 1987.

_____. *Education Theme Group Final Report.* 1988

_____. *Newsletter No. 2.* 1988.

_____. *Newsletter No. 3.* 1988.

_____. *Minutes to City Council Meeting.* 12 December 1988.

_____. *Minutes to City Council Meeting.* 14 August 1989.

_____. *Minutes to City Council Meeting.* 13 November 1989.

_____. *Comment Log.* 1989

_____. *Minutes to City Council Meeting.* 24 September 1990.

_____. *Minutes to City Council Meeting.* 14 December 1992.

_____. *Minutes to City Council Meeting.* 26 April 1993.

_____. *Minutes to City Council Meeting.* 4 May 1993.

_____. *Minutes to City Council Meeting.* 25 April 1994.

_____. *Minutes to City Council Meeting.* 14 December 1998.

_____. *City Manager's 1999 Budget Message.* 30 December 1998.

_____. *Rock Hill City Government Home Page.*
<http://www.ci.rock-hill.sc.us/history.htm> 18 October 2000.

Crosby, Barbara C. "Leading in a Shared- Power World." Pp. 613-631
in *Handbook of Public Administration.* 2nd ed. edited by James
L. Perry. San Francisco: Jossey-Bass, 1996.

Dahl, Robert. *Who Governs?* New Haven: Yale University Press, 1961.

Daly, Matthew. "A Place for the 1990s' Plan Would Renew Downtown
Rock Hill." *The Charlotte Observer-York*, 13 December 1987:
1(D), 2(D).

_____. "Rock Hill Chamber Reorganizes to Get 'Out Front.'" *The
Charlotte Observer-York*, 16 December 1987: B1

_____. "Preservation Key to Revitalization, Rock Hill Told." *The
Charlotte Observer-York*, 13 May 1988: 1(A).

_____. "Rock Hill Studies Greenway." *The Charlotte Observer-
York*, 20 July 1988: (1Y).

_____. "Rock Hill's Next Step: Sell District Plan to Voters. *The
Charlotte Observer-York*, 11 September 1988: 1, 15.

DeLeon, Richard E. *Left Coast City.* Lawrence, KS: University of
Kansas Press, 1992.

Denhardt, Robert B. "Strategic Planning in State and Local
Government." *State and Local Government Review* 17, no.1
(1985): 174-179.

Dozier, Al. "Campaign Ads Strike Nerve." *The Herald*, 31 October
1997: 1.

Eadie, Douglas C. "Putting a Powerful Tool to Practical Use: The
Application of Strategic Planning in the Public Sector." *Public
Administration Review* 43, no. 5 (September/October 1983):
447-52.

Echols, Doug. Personal Communication. September 21, 1999.

Editorial. "Does the Private Sector Share Planners' Vision?" *The Herald*, 29 May 1990: 6A.

Elkins, Ken. "Development Director Says City-Funded Study 'Politically Motivated.'" *The Herald*, 16 November 1995.

Faerman, Sue R. "Managing Conflicts Creatively." Pp. 632-646 in *Handbook of Public Administration*. 2nd ed. edited by James L. Perry. San Francisco: Jossey-Bass. 1996.

Ferman, Barbara. *Challenging the Growth Machine: Neighborhood Politics in Chicago and Pittsburgh*. Lawrence, KS: University of Kansas Press, 1996.

Francaviglia, Richard V. *Main Street Revisited*. Iowa City: The University of Iowa Press, 1996.

Garfield, Ken, "Haves Help the Have-Nots Empower Their Own Vision." *The Charlotte Observer-York*, 13 July 1990: 1(Y).

Gazella, Kim. "Rock Hill Shares Vision." *The Charlotte Observer-York,* 27 September 1989: 1(Y).

_____. "Council Agrees to let Architect Aid Rock Hill's Renovation." *The Charlotte Observer-York*, 10 April 1990.

Gill, Maxine. Personal Communication. September 21, 1999.

Goldfield, David R. and Blaine A. Brownell. *Urban America: A History*. 2nd Edition. Boston: Houghton Mifflin Company, 1990.

Goldfield, David R. "Urbanization in a Rural Culture." Pp. 67-93 in *The South for New Southerners*. Edited by Paul D. Escott and David R. Goldfield. Chapel Hill: The University of North Carolina Press, 1991.

_____. "The City as Southern History: The Past and The Promise of Tomorrow." Pp. 11-48 in *The Future of the South: A Historical Perspective for the Twenty-first Century*, edited by Joe P. Dunn and Howard L. Preston. Urbana: University of Illinois Press, 1991.

Golembieswki, Robert T. 1996. "The Future of Public Administration: End of a Short Stay in the Sun? Or a New Day A-Dawning." *Public Administration Review* 56, no. 2 (March April 1996): 139-148.

Gordon, Gerald L. *Strategic Planning in Local Government*. Washington, DC: International City/County Management Association, 1993.

Gustin, Nicole. "City in Debt $89 Million." *The Herald*, 21 September 1997: 1.

Hall, John Stuart and Louis F. Weschler. "The Phoenix Futures Forum:
    Creating Vision, Implanting Community." *National Civic
    Review* 80 (Spring 1990): 135-157.

Handal, Chris. "Mayor Says All citizens Can Have Say in Rock Hill's
    Future." *The Herald*, 8 March 1988: 1(A), 10(A).

_____. "Older City Structures Surveyed." *The Herald*, 3 April
    1988: 1A, 8A.

_____. "Rock Hill Aims to be No. 5 in S.C." *The Herald*, 4 April
    1988: 1A, 6A.

_____. "Winthrop, Rock Hill Can Set Example for Nation: Dean."
    The Herald, 19 July 1988: 1A.

_____. "To Work Magic, Take the Risk, Cultural Director tells
    Group." *The Herald*, 27 July 1988: 27, 1A.

_____. "Architect to Speak on Plan for Paths Linking City's Parks."
    The Herald, 2 August 1988: 1A.

_____. "Theater Consultant to Speak." *The Herald*, 10 August
    1988: 6A.

_____. "Offices Key to Downtown: Consultant." *The Herald*, 24
    August 1988: 1A.

_____. "Architect Unveils Downtown Plans." *The Herald*, 26
    August 1988: 1A, 8A.

_____. "Vision Farsighted, Officials Say." *The Herald*, 27, August
    1988: 1A, 8A.

_____. "Resident's Ideas on City Plan Sought." *The Herald*, 3
    September 1988: 1A.

_____. "Single-member Districts Approved." *The Herald*, 26 April
    1989: 1A.

_____. "Empowering the Vision leaders Get Ready for Action."
    The Herald, 7 May 1989: 1A.

_____. "Vision Leaders Pledge Commitment." *The Herald*, 14 May
    1989: 1A, 9A.

_____. "Snapshots of the Future." *The Herald*, 23 March 1990: 1A,
    8A

_____. "Downtown 'Vision' Tab: $11 Million." *The Herald*, 27
    May 1990: 1A, 14A.

_____. "Council to Review Spending Proposal." *The Herald*, 21
    July 1990: 4A.

_____. "Council Oks Bed-Tax Guidelines, 16.2 Million Bond
    Issue." *The Herald*, 24 July 1990: 4A.

_____. "City Council to Consider Higher Wrecker Fee." *The
    Herald*, 11 August 1990: 4A.

_____. "As Gateway Rises, So Do Visions of New City." The
      Herald, 30 September 1990: 1A, 14A.
_____. "School Board's Decision Affects Downtown Plan." The
      Herald, 30 October 1991: 5A.
_____. and Harrison, Cal. "Schools, County Seek Galleria Tax."
      The Herald, 16 August 1991: 1A.
Harper, Don. "RHEDC Embarks on Tenth Year." The Herald, 30
      January 1992.
Harrison, Cal. "Analysts Credit NCMPA's Rating to Growth,
      Management." The Herald, 31 July 1995.
Helling, Amy. "Collaborative Visioning: Proceed with Caution!:
      Results from Evaluating Atlanta's Vision 2020 Project."
      Journal of the American Planning Association 64, no. 3
      (1998): 335-340.
Hill, Susan. "Businesses Charged Up Over City's Power Rates." The
      Herald, 14 June 1994: 1A.
_____. "City: Accountant's Suggestions Nothing New." The
      Herald, 11 October 1994.
Himmelman, Arthur T. "Communities Working Collaboratively For a
      Change." Pp. 27-47 in Resolving Conflict: Strategies for Local
      Government, edited by Margaret S. Herrman. Washington,
      DC: International City/County Management Association,
      1994.
Hult. Karen M. and Charles Walcott. Governing Public Organizations:
      Politics,Structures, and Institutional Design. Pacific Grove,
      CA: Brooks/Cole Publishing, 1990.
Innes, Judith E. "Planning through Consensus Building: A New View of
      the Comprehensive Planning Ideal." Journal of the American
      Planning Association 62, no. 4 (1996): 460-473.
Jackson, Kenneth T. Crabgrass Frontier: The Suburbanization of the
      United States. New York: Oxford University Press, 1985.
Judd, Dennis R. and Todd Swanstrom. City Politics: Private Power and
      Public Policy. New York: HarperCollins College Publishers,
      1994.
Judge, Peter M. "Three Counties Tied Together in History." The
      Herald, 3 March 1989.
Kaufman, Jerome L. and Harvey M. Jacobs. "A Public Planning
      Perspective on Strategic Planning." Journal of the American
      Planning Association 53 (Winter 1987): 23-33.
Lanford, Joe. Personal Communication. 1990.
_____. Personal Communication. September 20, 1999.

Longshaw, Judy H. "Council Narrowly OKs Grant for Park." *The Herald*, 15 November 1994: 1.
_____. "3 Seats Up for Vote." *The Herald*, 15 October 1995.
_____. "City Tries to Wean Self from Utility." *The Herald*, 11 November 1995.
_____. "Further Study Ordered for Downtown Plan." *The Herald*, 19 March 1996.
_____. "Group Taking Notes About City's Future." *The Herald*, 15 August 1996.
_____. "Echols Elected Rhea's Successor." *The Herald*, 5 November 1997: 1A, 9A.
Mauldin, Doug. "Price for Gateway, Civitas at Least $1.27 Million, Official Says." *The Herald*, 17 April 1991.
_____. "Developer Fears Park Will Boost Rates." *The Herald*, 29 March 1992: 10A.
_____. "City Rejects Petitions for Bond Referendum." *The Herald*, 19 November 1992
_____. "Arts Council Wants City as Partner." *The Herald*, 27 January 1993.
_____. "Rock Hill to get Star Treatment." *The Herald*, 13 July 1996.
McClendon, Bruce W. and John A. Lewis. "Goals for Corpus Christi: Citizen Participation in Planning." *National Civic Review* (February 1985): 72-80.
McGuire, Justin. "Rock Hill Councilwoman Defends Ward Seat." The Herald, 12 October 1999: 1.
_____. "Incumbents Gill, Sutton Re-Elected." *The Herald*, 20 October 1999: 1.
McGuire, Michael, Barry Rubin, Robert Agranoff, and Craig Richards. "Building Development Capacity in NonMetropolitan Communities." *Public Administration Review* 54, no. 5 (1994): 426-433.
McKenzie, Susan. "Turner's Vision Tied to City's Past." *The Herald*, 25 October 1993: 6B.
Merrell, Dennis. Personal Communication. September 23, 1999.
Milstead. David. "County Files Suit Against Rock Hill." *The Herald*, 2 January 1999: A1.
Morrill, Jim. "Two Blacks Win Council Primary." *The Herald*, 17 October 1979: 1
Most, Doug. "Spratt, Arts Council Can Keep Offices." *The Herald*, 9

February 1993.

National Civic League. *The Civic Index*. Denver, CO: The National
Civic League, 1999.

Okubo, Derek, *The Community Visioning and Strategic Planning
Handbook*. Denver, CO: The National Civic League Press,
1997.

Palmetto Benchmarking Project. *Survey Results for the City of Rock
Hill*. Columbia, SC: Institute of Public Affairs, University of
South Carolina, 1998.

Parr, John and David Lampe. "Empowering Citizens." Pp. 196-209 in
Handbook of Public Administration. 2nd ed. edited by James L.
Perry. San Francisco: Jossey-Bass, 1996.

Parris, Lou. "Jerome Stays in: Gill, Berry Out." *The Herald*, 21 October
1981: 1, 3.

Pecorella, Robert. *Community Power in a Post Reform City*. Armonk,
NY: M.E. Sharpe, 1994.

Peterson, Paul E. "Forms of Representation: Participation of the Poor in
the Community Action Program." *American Political Science
Review* 64 (June 1970): 491-507.

Pettibon, Sula S. "Rhea Wins Mayoral Primary." *The Herald*, 16
October 1985: 1, 18.

Pilla, Jen. "Social Advocate Gill Files for Full Term on Council."
Charlotte Observer-York Edition, 27 July 1999: 1Y, 3Y.
_____. "Sutton Files to Keep Seat on Rock Hill City Council."
Charlotte Observer-York Edition, 27 July 1999: 1Y, 3Y.

Pitkin, Hannah. *The Concept of Representation*. Berkeley: University of
California Press. 1967.

Poister, Theodore H. and Gregory Streib. "Management Tools in
Municipal Government: Trends over the Past Decade." *Public
Administration Review* 49, no. 3(1989): 240-248.

Potapchuk, William R. "New Approaches to Citizen Participation:
Building Consent." *National Civic Review* 80 (Spring 1990):
158-168.
_____. Jarle P. Crocker, Dina Boogaard, and William H. Schechter.
*Building Community: Exploring the Role of Social Capital
and Local Government*. Washington, DC: Program for
Community Problem Solving, 1998.

Potapchuk, William R. "Building an Infrastructure of Community
Collaboration." *National Civic Review* 88, no. 3 (1999): 165-
169.
_____. Jarle P. Crocker, and William H. Schechter. "The

Transformative Power of Governance." *National Civic Review*
88, no. 3 (1999): 217-247.

Price, Mark. "Schools Accept Tax Deal." *Charlotte Observer-York
Edition*, 6 September 1991: 1Y.

Putnam, Robert D. "Bowling Alone: America's Declining Social
Capital." *Journal of Democracy* 6, no. 1 (1995): 65-78.

Reed, Christine M., B.J. Reed, and Jeffrey S.Luke. "Assessing
Readiness for Economic Development Strategic Planning."
Journal of the American Planning Association 53 (Autumn
1987): 521-530.

Reichardt, Charles S., and Thomas D. Cook. "Beyond Qualitative
Versus Quantitative Methods." Pp. 7-32 in *Qualitative and
Quantitative Methods in Evaluation Research*, edited by T.
Cook and C. Reichardt. Beverly Hills, CA: Sage Publications,
1979.

Rhea, Betty Jo. Personal Communication. September 22, 1999.

Rider, Robert W. "Making Strategic Planning Work in Local
Government." *Long Range Planning* 16 (June 1983): 73-81.

Rock Hill Economic Development Corporation. *Annual Report.* 1991

Roddey, Osbey. Personal Communication. September 29, 1999.

Rohe, William M. and Lauren B. Gates. *Planning with Neighborhoods.*
Chapel Hill: University of North Carolina Press, 1985.

Savitch, H.V. and Thomas, John Clayton. "Conclusion: End of the
Millennium Big City Politics." Pp. 235-251 in *Big City
Politics in Transition*, edited by H.V. Savitch and John
Clayton Thomas. Newbury Park: Sage Publications, 1991.

Searles, Winston. Personal Communication. September 22, 1999.

Scavo, Carmen. "The Use of Participative Mechanisms by Large
American Cities." *Journal of Urban Affairs* 15 (1993): 93-
109.

Scott, Patrick. "Rock Hill Passes its Fiscal Exam." The *Charlotte
Observer-York*, 30 October 1995: 1Y, 3Y.

Simpson, Chad. "City, County Settle Suit." *The Herald*, 29 July 1999:
1A.

Sorkin, Donna L., Nancy B. Ferris, and James Hudak. *Strategies for
Cities and Counties: A Strategic Planning Guide.* Washington,
DC: Public Technology, Inc, 1984.

Sparrow, Glen W. "The Emerging Chief Executive 1971-1991: A San
Diego Update." Pp. 187-199 in *Facilitative Leadership in
Local Government*, edited by James H. Svara. San Francisco:
Sage Publications, 1994.

Staff Reports. "School Board Rejects Galleria Tax District." *The Herald*, 30 August 1991: 1A.

Stoker, Gerry. 1995. "Regime Theory and Urban Politics." Pp. 96-116 in *Theories of Urban Politics*, edited by David Judge, Gerry Stoker, and Harold Wolman. London: Sage Publications, 1995.

Stone, Clarence N. *Regime Politics*. Lawrence, KS: University of Kansas Press, 1989.

_____. Orr, Marion E. and Imbroscio, David. "The Reshaping of Urban Leadership in U.S. Cities: A Regime Analysis." Pp. 222-239 in *Urban Life in Transition*, edited by M. Gottdiener and Chris G. Pickvance. Newbury Park: Sage Publications, 1991.

Streib, Gregory and Theodore H. Poister. "The Use of Strategic Planning in Municipal Governments." Pp. 18-25 in *The Municipal Year Book 2002*, Washington, DC: International City/County Management Association, 2002.

Sutton, Kevin. Personal Communication. September 21, 1999.

Svara, James H. *Official Leadership in the City*. New York: Oxford University Press, 1990.

_____. and Associates. *Facilitative Leadership in Local Government*. San Francisco: Jossey-Bass Publishers, 1994.

_____.. Svara, "Mayors in the Unity of Powers Context: Effective Leadership in Council-Manager Governments," Pp. 43-54 in *The Future of Local Government Administration*, eds. H. George Frederickson and John Nalbandian, Washington, DC: International City/County Management Association, 2002.

Thomas, John Clayton. *Public Participation in Public Decisions*. San Francisco: Jossey-Bass, 1995.

Thomas, Ronald L., Mary C. Means, and Margaret Grieve. *Taking Charge: How Communities Are Planning their Futures*. Washington, DC: International City Management Association, 1988.

U.S. Department of Commerce. U.S. Census of Population 1980. Washington, DC: Bureau of the Census, 1980.

_____. U.S. Census of Population 2000. Washington, DC: Bureau of the Census, 2000.

Walker, Andrea K. "Sutton and Echols Unleash Attack Ads." *Charlotte Observer-York Edition*, 31 October 1997: 1Y, 4Y.

_____. "In Rock Hill Mayor's Race, Money's the Main Issue.'*Charlotte Observer-York Edition*, 2 November 1997:

1Y, 5Y.

_____. "Vision Unveiled for City of Dreams." *Charlotte Observer-York Edition*, 27 May 1988: 1Y, 3Y.

_____. "Chamber Chief Foresees a Rock Hill Explosion as Growth Continues." *Charlotte Observer-York Edition*, 2 January 1999: 1Y, 3Y.

_____. "City Envisions Saluda Street Revival." *Charlotte Observer-York Edition*, 8 January 1999: 1Y, 3Y.

Walsh, Mary. *Building Citizen Involvement: Strategies for Local Government*. Washington, DC: International City/County Management Association, 1997.

Weeks, Edmund C. "The Practice of Deliberative Democracy: Results from Four Large-Scale Trials." *Public Administration Review* 60, no. 4 (July/August 2000): 360-372.

Wheeland, Craig M. 1991. "Empowering the Vision: Citywide Strategic Planning." *National Civic Review* 80, no. 4 (Fall 1991): 393-405.

_____. "Citywide Strategic Planning: An Evaluation of Rock Hill's Empowering the Vision." *Public Administration Review* 53, no. 1 (January/ February 1993): 65-72.

_____. "A Profile of a Facilitative Mayor: Mayor Betty Jo Rhea of RockHill, SC." Pp. 136-159 in *Facilitative Leadership in Local Government*, edited by James H. Svara. San Francisco: Sage Publications, 1994.

_____. "Implementing a Community-Wide Strategic Plan: Rock Hill's Empowering the Vision Ten Years Later." *The American Review of Public Administration*. 33, no. 1 (March 2003): 46-69.

White, Sally. "Skeptical About Downtown Plan." *The Herald*, 29 May 1989.

Wilson, James Q. "Planning and Politics: Citizen Participation in Urban Renewal." Pp. 407-421 in *Urban Renewal: The Record and the Controversy*, edited by James Q. Wilson, ed. Cambridge, MA: M.I.T. Press, 1966.

Wood, Donna J. and Barbara Gray. "Toward a Comprehensive Theory of Collaboration." *Journal of Applied Behavioral Science* 27, no. 2 (1991): 139-62

Woodmansee, Jason. "Community Visioning: Citizen Participation in Strategic Planning." *MIS Report 26(3)*. Washington, DC: International City/County Management Association, 1994.

Index

Aberman, Eddie, 92
Airport Industrial Park, 92
Allen, Russell, xi, 46-48, 52,
    67-68, 70-71, 95, 100-101, 195
Andrew, Clay, 93-94
anti-regime, 8
Arts Council, 60, 85, 89-91
at-large elections, 86
Ayers, Sylvia, 72

Barber, Nate, 72
Baxter Hood Continuing
    Education Center, 60
Bazemore, Jim, 90
Belk, Bob, 16, 72
Berry, Frank, 87
Belk building, 22-24, 33-34, 38,
    41, 55, 110
Bigham, Larry, 81
Bigham, Kathy, 81-82
Blue, Gilbert, 48
Botsch, Julie, Acknowledgements
Boyd Hill, 40
Burt, Joann, 48
business arena, 9-10, 107
Business City, 4, 17, 20, 25, 32
business parks, 4, 42, 49, 53, 61,
    68, 70, 73, 81, 92-94

Campbell, Lynn, 18
caretaker (regime), 8, 97, 101, 105
Carter, Andy, 16
Catawba Indian Nation, 47-49,
    53-54
Catawba Regional Planning
    Council, 17
CDBG, see Community

Development Block Grant
Center for the Arts, 89, 98
Central Rock Hill Plan, 24-26
charettes, 14, 21-22, 27, 33, 42
Charlotte MSA, see Charlotte,
    North Carolina Metropolitan
    Statistical Area
Charlotte, North Carolina
    Metropolitan Statistical Area,
    2-4, 15, 19-21
Cherry Park, 15, 67, 70, 91
Citizens for Rock Hill's Future,
    49, 96
city council, 34, 46, 52, 60, 66-67,
    69, 83, 87-89, 98, 100-101,
    105, 107, 110
City Hall, 60, 82
city manager(s), 2, 6, 14, 42, 52,
    65-66, 101, 105, 106
City of Rock Hill, 4, 16, 25, 41,
    48, 54, 61
civic arena, 9-10, 107
civic infrastructure, 63
Civitas, 60
Clinton Junior College, 2, 20
collaborative decision-making, 6,
    42, 45, 49, 64
Colter, Tom, 83
Committee for a Better Rock Hill,
    90-91
community-building, 2
Community Development Block
    Grant (CDBG), 41, 60, 74, 92
community-wide plans, see
    community-wide strategic
    planning
community-wide strategic plan,

see community-wide strategic
planning
community-wide strategic
planning, Preface, 1-2, 4-6, 10-
11, 15, 29-30, 32, 34, 42, 47,
49-50, 52, 56-57, 59, 62-64,
70-71, 88, 101, 103-105, 107,
111
computer-generated images, 6, 23,
33-34
consultant(s), 6, 32-34, 42, 49,
104
conservatives, 55, 69, 71, 81-83,
85-95, 97-101
Cook Vicki Huggins, 18, 72
Cope, Marty, 16, 72
Corley, Charles, 18
Corporatist (regime), 8, 107
council-manager, 2
Crawford Road, 15, 38, 40-41, 87
Crump, Herb, 100
Cultural City, 4, 17, 20, 25, 32, 36

Dalton, Harry, 18, 72
Dave Lyle Boulevard, 23, 34, 60,
70, 78, 89
Davenport, Jane, 82, 98
deindustrialization, 3, 107
DeMarcus, W. Mark, 72
development coalition, 3
DiGiorgio, Anthony, 48
Doswell, Marshall, 18, 72
downtown, see downtown
business district
downtown business district, 3, 20,
22-23, 49, 59, 68, 70, 73, 76,
83, 88, 90-91, 93-94, 99-100,
103-106

Echols, Doug, xi, 46, 52, 67-
68, 71, 82-83, 98-99, 105
economic development strategy, 4,
94
Educational City, 4, 17, 20, 25, 32
Eggleston, Jewell, 98

electoral arena, 9-11, 107
electric utility, 49, 55, 78, 81-82,
85, 94-96, 99, 101, 106
elitist (regime), 8, 107
elitists, 7
Elliot, Carl (Buzz), 48, 72
Emmett Scott Neighborhood
Center, 87
Empowering the Community
(ETC), 4-5, 47-50, 52-55, 57-
58, 61-63, 67, 75, 82, 82, 99-
101, 104-105, 107, 110-111
Empowering the Vision (ETV),
Preface, 2, 4-6, 10, 14, 16, 18,
20-24, 29-38, 40-42, 45-50,
52-55, 57-64, 67, 71, 73, 75,
81-83, 85-86, 88, 90-91, 93-94,
97-101, 104-107, 109-114
Enterprise Fund, see electric
utility
ETC, see Empowering the
Community
ETV, see Empowering the Vision
ETV staff, 14, 17, 34, 109

facilitative mayor, 66-67
Fagan, Tom, 100
Finley, Gwendolyn, 98-99
Flint Hill, 40
First Union National Bank, 41
focal point plans, 14-15
Functional City, 4, 17, 20, 25, 32
Garden City, 4, 17, 20, 25, 32, 36
Gardner, Cecelia, 72
Gateway (Plaza) Project, 23, 42,
60, 82, 88-89, 91, 98, 100
general public, 14, 24, 47, 52, 55,
71, 75
Gentry, Joe, 16, 74
George, Buck, 48
Gill, Johnny, 18
Gill, Maxine, 81, 90, 98, 101
governance, 2, 6, 62
governance network, 7, 45, 63,
104

growth machines, 9
Gullick, Carl, 48

Hardin, Jim, 72, 96
Harper, Don, 72
Harrelson, Hugh, 81, 87-89, 91-93, 98-99
Herlong/Ebenezer Road, 15
Herron, Rob, 99-101
Hipp, C. John, 72
Historic City, 4, 17, 19, 25, 32, 36
Historic Review Board, 60
Holland, Max, 66
Honeycutt, H. Butch, 72
Hood, Baxter, 16
Hornsby, Clarence, 18, 48, 72
Houston, Vince, 81, 95
hyperpluralist (regime), 8, 107

I-77 Corridor Plan, 61, 100
idea forms, 24
initial agreement, 14
intergovernmental arena, 9-10, 107
Ivey, Bidwell, 81, 88-91, 93, 97-98, 101

James, Barbara, 72
Jerome, J. Emmett, 66, 81-82, 92
Jubilee: Festival of the Arts, 60, 89

Kelly, Phil, 74
Killian, Clay, 48
Kimmel, Manning, 72, 96
Klugh, Gene, 16
Knox, Paul, 98
KPMG Peat Marwick, 93, 96

Lanford, Joe, xi, 3, 14-17, 20-22, 27, 30, 32-34, 41, 46, 52, 66-67, 71, 90-91, 95, 98, 101, 105-106
living plan, 23, 27, 41

lower-class opportunity (regime), 8-9, 106
Lyle, Dave, 66, 82,90

Mack, Bayles, 48
Mallaney, Bob, 18
Marcovitz, Melisa, xi
mayor(s), 6, 42, 52, 65-67, 69, 101, 105-106
McDaniel, Phillip, 58
McMillan, Becky, 16
Melton, Ted, 16, 48
Merrell, Dennis, 16, 48, 62
middle-class progressive (regime), 8, 10-11, 41, 65, 67-68, 83, 88, 97, 101, 105-107
Minicozzi, Anne, xi
Mitchell, Barre, 48, 72
Model Cities Program, 70
models, 14, 23, 41, 55
Morgan-Adams Group, 23, 34
Mozzone, Diane, xi
Municipal Association of South Carolina Achievement Award, 6
Murphy, Mary, xi

neighborhood empowerment, 5, 47, 61
Neighborhood Improvement Program, 41
Neel, Bill, 99
Neely, Bill, 16, 72
Norman, Ralph, 81, 93-95
Norman, Warren, 81, 93-95
North Cherry Road Development Project, 70, 74, 100

Owen, J. Hank, 48

participatory structures, 56-57
Patrick, Wayne, 72
Peeples, Jane, 48
Pharr, John, 81
physical models, 6, 23, 33

Piedmont, 2-3
Piedmont Municipal Power
    Agency (PMPA), 70, 95-97
Piper, Martha Kime, 15-16
Plumb, Terry, 72
Pluralist (regime), 8-10, 41, 65,
    67-68, 70, 83, 101,105-107
pluralists, 7
PMPA, see Piedmont Municipal
    Power Agency
Porter, Annie, 32, 34
Porter Road, 41
process champions, 6, 31-32
progressives, 52, 55, 69-71, 73,
    75-76, 82-83, 85-88, 91, 93-
    101, 103-106
project coordinator, 19, 31-32, 42,
    107

Raiburn, Gail, xi
Rast, Steve, 82-83, 90-91
redevelopment (regime), 8, 10-11,
    65-68, 88-97-101,105
Reese, Jim, 16
Reno, Jim, 99-101
Rhea, Elizabeth (Betty) Jo,
    xi, 3, 15-17, 22, 24, 26-27, 30,
    34, 46-48, 52, 66-68, 71, 73,
    82-83, 87, 91, 93, 95, 98, 105
Rhea, Grazier, 18, 72
ring city, 3, 21
RHEDC, see Rock Hill Economic
    Development Corporation
River Park, 61, 70, 74
Rock Hill (Area) Chamber of
    Commerce, 4, 10, 15-16, 19-
    20, 22, 25, 48-49, 53-54, 59,
    71, 76, 78, 91-92, 94
Rock Hill Council of
    Neighborhoods, 62
Rock Hill Economic Development
    Corporation (RHEDC),
    Preface, 4, 10, 16, 18, 25, 46-
    48, 53-55, 60-61, 70-71, 74,
    81, 85, 87, 89, 91-94, 96, 100,

110
Rock Hill Joint Venture on
    Affordable Housing, 60
Rock Hill School District No. 3, 4,
    10, 15-16, 19-20, 25, 48, 53-
    54, 59, 71, 73-74, 94
Rock Hill-York County Airport,
    61
Roddey, Osbey, 48, 52, 71, 87,
    98-101
Rogers, David, 72
Rogers, Tom, 99

Saluda Street, 87
Schaller, Rachel, xi
Scoville, Charlie, 18
Searles, Winston, 52, 71, 82, 87,
    97-101
Shapiro, Gerald, 26
Simpson, James, 72
Smith, Carey, 101
Smith, Michael, 16
social development strategy, 4
South Carolina Association of
    Planners Award, 6
Southway Industrial Park, 92
Southern urban village, 4, 42
special events, 14, 19
Springs Industry, 22
stakeholders, 6, 30, 56, 59, 104
steering committee, 4, 14-15, 17,
    24-27, 34, 37, 41, 47, 54, 57,
    63, 104, 109
strategic leadership, 11
strategic planning, 1, 5-6, 13-14,
    27, 29, 31-33, 40, 42, 45-46,
    49, 55, 104, 107
structuralists, 7
Stuber, Dennis, 72
Sutton, Kevin, 67, 81-82, 88, 98-
    101
symbolic setting, 6, 42

tax increment district, see tax
    increment financing

tax increment financing, 64, 70,
    73, 81, 89, 93-94
TechPark, 73, 89, 92
textile industry, 2, 3
The Herald (Rock Hill), Preface,
    34, 47, 55, 57, 71, 104, 109-
    110
theme group(s), 4, 14, 17-24, 27,
    31-32, 34, 36-37, 41, 47, 49,
    52-53, 55, 57-58, 71, 75, 104,
    109-111
Thomas, Bill, 81, 88, 91, 97-98,
    101
Thompson, Robert (Bob), 18, 48,
    72
Thomas, Marty, 100
Tisdale, Baxter, 83
timetable, 14, 24
TownCenter Mall, 10, 22, 42, 49,
    61, 70, 78, 82, 90, 92
Turner, Stephen, 48, 93
Tuttle, H. P. Skip, 72

urban arenas, 9
urban regime, 2, 7-9
urban regime theory, 7
urban sprawl, 3
U.S. Conference of Mayors
    Livability Award, 6

Vaughn, Lud, 72
Vipperman, David, 16, 48, 72
visionary leadership, 104-106

Walker, Paul, 81, 95
Warner, Jimmy, 100
Warren, Wanda, 48
Waterford Business Park, 61, 73-
    74, 82, 92-94
Whitehead, Greg, 82
Wilson, Melford, 66, 71
Wingate, Wayne, 18
Winthrop College (University),
    Preface, 2, 4, 15-17, 19-20, 22,
    47-48, 53-54, 59, 61, 71

Woods, Henry, 52, 71, 97

York County, 4, 10, 15-16, 19,
    25-26, 48, 53-54, 59-61, 71,
    73-74, 94, 99
York County Regional Chamber
    of Commerce, see Rock Hill
    (Area) Chamber of Commerce
York Tech, see York Technical
    College
York Technical College, 4, 16, 20,
    22, 25, 48, 53-54, 61, 71

About the Author

Craig M. Wheeland is associate professor of political science at Villanova University. He received a BA in history from the University of South Carolina at Aiken, an MPA from the University of South Carolina and a Ph.D. in political science from The Pennsylvania State University. He currently serves as Chair of the Department of Political Science and directs Villanova's MPA program. He is past president of the Pennsylvania Political Science Association and past president of the Northeastern Political Science Association. His research interests include leadership by elected officials and professional administrators in city and suburban governments; collaborative problem-solving approaches, and municipal government institutions. Professor Wheeland has published several book chapters and his journal articles have appeared in *Public Administration Review*, *Administration & Society*, *American Review of Public Administration*, *Public Productivity & Management Review*, *State and Local Government Review*, *Public Integrity*, *National Civic Review*, among others.